THE HATE U GIVE

Angie Thomas

AUTHORED by

COVER DESIGN by Table XI Partners LLC
COVER PHOTO by Olivia Verma and © 2005 GradeSaver, LLC

BOOK DESIGN by Table XI Partners LLC

Copyright © 2017 GradeSaver LLC

Published by GradeSaver LLC, www.gradesaver.com

First published in the United States of America by GradeSaver LLC. 2017

GRADESAVER, the GradeSaver logo and the phrase "Getting you the grade since 1999" are registered trademarks of GradeSaver, LLC

ISBN 978-1-60259-905-5

Printed in the United States of America

For other products and additional information please visit http://www.gradesaver.com

Table of Contents

Biography of Angie Thomas

Angie Thomas claims that before the publication of *The Hate U Give*, her greatest accomplishment was an article about her teenage rapping career published in *Right-On* magazine. *The Hate U Give* certainly knocked that accomplishment out of the park—it was a #1 New York Times Bestseller, acquired by the Balzer + Bray branch of HarperCollins publishers after a bidding war between 13 publishing houses. Since its publication, the book has received starred reviews from eight literary journals—a particularly high number for a young adult novel. Publications such as *The New York Times* and *Entertainment Weekly* have referred to the book as "required reading," and a film adaption starring *Hunger Games* actress Amandla Stenberg is in the works.

Angie Thomas was born, raised, and still resides in Jackson, Mississippi. In an interview, she recalled witnessing a shootout between two drug dealers at a local park. The next day, Thomas's mother took her to the library to show her that "there was more to the world than what I saw that day." Thomas has a passionate interest in race-related activism; she was inspired to right *The Hate U Give* in the wake of news coverage about the police shootings of unarmed black people as young as 12. In addition, Thomas saw that blackness is often portrayed in a negative light, and that the perspective of young black women is typically omitted from the national dialogue on police brutality and racial profiling—even though these women are frequently affected.

Thomas holds a BFA in Creative Writing from Belhaven University. She is the inaugural winner of the Walter Dean Myers Grant from the activist group We Need Diverse Books. Like her novel's protagonist Starr Carter, she is a fan of Tupac, sneakers, and Harry Potter.

The Hate U Give Study Guide

The Hate U Give, Angie Thomas's first novel, debuted as number one on *The New York Times* bestseller list when it was published in February 2017. Thomas developed the novel from a short story she wrote for her senior project in Belhaven University's creative writing program, shortly after the 2009 shooting of Oscar Grant. After graduating, Thomas set the project aside because of its emotionally taxing subject matter; the news of subsequent police shootings drew her back to the work. She received the Walter Dean Myers Grant from the activist group We Need Diverse Books to support her writing.

Thomas was concerned that publishers wouldn't be interested in the book because of its polarizing subject material; she asked literary agent Brooks Sherman if a Black Lives Matter-inspired book would be amenable to publishers via Twitter in June 2015. Thomas got a resounding answer to that question when the book set off a bidding war between 13 publishing houses.

The Hate U Give was a critical success, drawing praise in forums such as *Salon*, *Kirkus Reviews*, and *Publishers Weekly*. A movie adaption of the novel by 20th Century Fox is in the works, directed by George Tillman, Jr., with a screenplay by Audrey Wells and starring Amandla Stenberg.

Written from the viewpoint of a 16-year-old African-American girl, the novel deals directly with issues of police brutality, racial profiling, and activism. Its title is a nod to THUG LIFE—The Hate U Give Little Infants Fucks Everybody—an acronym coined by rapper Tupac Shakur that encapsulates the cyclical nature of crime, poverty, and hate as a result of racism.

The Hate U Give Summary

The novel opens on 16-year-old protagonist Starr Carter attending a spring break party with her friend, Kenya. Starr's family lives in Garden Heights, a predominantly black and impoverished urban neighborhood, but she and her brothers attend a ritzy and mostly white private school forty-five minutes away. At the party, Starr is acutely aware of the double-sided personality this lifestyle engenders: she tries not to act "ghetto" at school, but neighborhood kids accuse her of abandoning them for white friends. Starr has just started to catch up with Khalil—her best friend from childhood, who has entered the dangerous world of drug dealing since Starr began attending prep school—when a gang dispute leads to a dancefloor gunfight. Starr and Khalil flee the scene and are pulled over by a police officer for driving with a broken taillight. The officer pats Khalil down and walks back to his car. When Khalil opens his car door to ask Starr if she's okay, the officer opens fire, and Starr watches her friend die.

The grief, confusion, anger, and fear that Starr must deal with in the aftermath of Khalil's death make her initially unwilling to identify herself as the sole witness of the night's events. As time passes, however, she loses her reluctance, serving as part of the police department's investigation, speaking to the local defense attorney, and hiring a lawyer from a local activist group. Starr ultimately embraces activism herself by advocating for justice for Khalil on a nationally-televised interview and brazenly joining street protests after a grand jury fails to indict the officer who shot Khalil. Throughout the weeks that follow Khalil's death, Starr must grapple not only with her own guilt and trauma, but also with white classmates who use the event as an excuse to get out of class or imply that the officer had done society a favor by shooting a drug dealer. She hides her involvement from her Williamson friends and her white boyfriend, Chris, before the truth comes bubbling up and Starr realizes which of her friends are worth keeping.

The tragedy of Khalil's death tears through a neighborhood already fragmented by drugs and violence from deeply entrenched gangs. Starr's father, Maverick, is a former gang member who spent time in prison before he could extricate himself from the street life. His long-standing feud with Kenya's father, King—a gangster who effectively runs the neighborhood—puts Starr's family in constant danger. Tensions arise between Maverick and his brother-in-law Carlos; Carlos was Starr's first father figure while Maverick was locked up. The tense situation is further complicated because Carlos is a cop serving on the same force as the officer who shot Khalil. Torn between the protective impulse he feels for Starr and the loyalty he has towards his career, Carlos helps Starr see that police cannot be characterized as generally corrupt or bad people.

Starr's mother, Lisa, argues with Maverick about whether the family should move out of Garden Heights. At first, Maverick is opposed because he believes he can best improve Garden Heights when he is living in it; Lisa counters that their family's safety is a priority and that Maverick can continue to use the grocery store he owns in the neighborhood as a means to help the community. Ultimately, the family moves to the suburbs, but Starr's brother Seven—who lives with Kenya and King—remains torn between the urge to stay and protect his mother and sisters, and the desire to attend college outside of the city. Meanwhile, a newly initiated gangbanger named DeVante turns to Maverick for help in getting out of the gang; he ends up living with Carlos.

The tensions and feuds running through the novel come to a head with the grand jury decision over whether to arrest the officer who shot Khalil. When the jury fails to indict, protests and riots take over Garden Heights. King takes advantage of the chaos to set fire to Maverick's store while Starr, Chris, Seven, and DeVante are trapped inside. With Maverick's help, they manage to escape; the neighborhood turns on King, getting him arrested for arson. With the promise of Carlos's protection, DeVante agrees to serve as witness to King's drug-dealing schemes, removing him from the neighborhood's gang scene and ending his abuse towards Kenya and Seven's mother. Maverick also grows to accept Chris, inviting his daughter's boyfriend to go boxing with him. The novel ends with Starr making a promise to Khalil's memory: she won't remain silent, and will continue fighting against injustice.

The Hate U Give Characters

Starr Carter

Starr Carter is the novel's protagonist, a sixteen-year-old African-American living in the mostly poor and black neighborhood of Garden Heights while attending the upscale, largely-white private school Williamson Prep. When she was ten, Starr saw her friend Natasha killed in a drive-by shooting; the trauma of this experience is repeated at the beginning of the novel when Starr witnesses the death of her friend Khalil at the hands of a police officer. The novel follows Starr as she attempts to navigate the two worlds of Garden Heights and Williamson Prep while simultaneously dealing with grief over Khalil's death and her forays into activism in response to the unjust shooting.

Maverick "Big Mav" Carter

Maverick, Starr's father, owns and operates a grocery store in Garden Heights and is a firm believer in the tenets of Black Power espoused by Huey Newton. A former gangbanger, Maverick spent three years in prison before fatherhood inspired him to get out of the gang system. He supports Starr throughout the novel, inspiring her to not be silent in the face of injustice. Although he feuds with his brother-in-law and struggles to accept Starr's white boyfriend, by the end of the book Maverick makes peace with those who care about Starr.

Lisa Carter

Lisa, Starr's mother, is an invaluable source of support and care for her daughter throughout the novel. She encourages Starr to do as much as she is comfortable with in terms of activism and speaking out. Lisa worries for the safety of her family and convinces Maverick that their family should move out of the Garden Heights neighborhood. At the beginning of the book, she works as a nurse in a Garden Heights clinic, but she later secures a higher-paying job in a different hospital which makes the family's move financially feasible.

Seven

Seven is Starr's half-brother; Maverick is Seven's father, and Iesha, the gangbanger King's girlfriend, is his mother. Seven has a close relationship with Starr—they play basketball together every month, he drives her home from school every day—and he supports his sister during the difficult grieving period following Khalil's death. He's eighteen, and is accepted to many colleges, but doesn't want to leave Garden Heights because he feels the need to protect Iesha and his sisters from King's physical abuse. Ultimately, Maverick convinces Seven to pursue the opportunities open to him and attend a college outside of the city.

Sekani

Sekani is Starr's younger brother, who also attends Williamson Prep. At first, Starr's parents don't tell Sekani that Starr witnessed Khalil's death, but eventually tell him as Starr gets more involved with efforts to protest the shooting. Starr and Sekani frequently have good-natured fights and bicker with each other.

Chris

Chris is Starr's boyfriend. He shares Starr's love for Jordan sneakers and *The Fresh Prince of Bel-Air.* However, he's also rich and white; Starr feels that this creates distance between them, while Chris insists that Starr let him into the side of her life she usually tries to hide from her Williamson friends. Although Maverick doesn't accept Chris at first, the two grow closer throughout the novel.

Hailey Grant

Hailey is one of Starr's friends at Williamson Prep. At the beginning of the novel, their friendship is strained because Hailey unfollowed Starr's Tumblr account after Starr posted a picture of Emmett Till, a fourteen-year-old black boy murdered for whistling at a white woman. Hailey doesn't redeem herself throughout the novel, either; she insinuates that Khalil is better off dead because he sold drugs, and she repeatedly makes racist comments to Starr while denying that she herself is a racist. The tension between the two friends builds until they get into a physical altercation at school. At the end of the book, Starr decides to cut Hailey out of her life, since the negative aspects of the friendship outweigh the positive.

Maya Yang

Maya is one of Starr's closest friends at Williamson. Like Starr, Maya plays for the school's basketball team. She also lives on Carlos's street. Maya is Asian-American, and when Hailey makes racist comments about Maya's ethnicity, Maya and Starr agree to make a "minority alliance" and refuse to allow Hailey to make prejudiced remarks towards them.

Kenya

Kenya is one of Starr's friends who lives in Garden Heights. She and Starr share a brother, since Maverick is Seven's father and Iesha is the mother of both Kenya and Seven. Kenya has an outsized personality and isn't afraid to fight people, but she also calls Starr out for not speaking up for Khalil as she believes Khalil would have if their roles were reversed. In addition, Kenya has to deal with physical abuse from King.

King

King is the most notorious gangbanger in the neighborhood, a King Lord deeply involved in drug dealing and violent acts. When Maverick took a prison charge and saved King from getting locked up, King allowed Maverick to leave the King Lords. King is also abusive towards his girlfriend, Iesha, and to his kids, Kenya, Seven, and Lyric. The neighborhood ultimately turns on King, turning him in to the police after he sets fire to Maverick's store.

Iesha

Iesha is King's girlfriend and the mother of Seven, Kenya, and Lyric. Although Seven and Iesha have a strained relationship because Seven believes that she doesn't reciprocate his love—she didn't even show up to his high school graduation—Iesha makes sacrifices for Seven as well. She is a point of contention in Maverick and Lisa's relationship, because Maverick conceived Seven with her after having a fight with Lisa.

DeVante

DeVante is a teenager who lives in Garden Heights and ends up getting involved with the King Lords. He joins the gang and sells drugs in an attempt to find a kind of family and to make money to provide for his mother and brother. Fearing that he will end up dead or in prison, DeVante turns to Maverick for help in getting out of the King Lords. Maverick sends him to live at Carlos's house. At the end of the novel, DeVante agrees to turn witness against King to protect Iesha, Seven, Kenya, Lyric, and the Garden Heights community.

Khalil

Khalil, Starr's best friend from childhood, is shot while unarmed by a police officer who had pulled him over for having a broken taillight. Although Khalil's death occurs in the first few pages of the novel, his presence reverberates throughout the novel. Khalil sold drugs because his mother, Brenda—who struggles with addiction—was in debt to King. King tried to persuade Khalil to join the King Lords, but Khalil refused.

Carlos

Carlos, who is Lisa's brother, serves as a police officer in the same force with the officer who shot Khalil. When Maverick was in prison—from when Starr was three years old until she was six—Carlos served as a father figure to Starr. This creates tension between him and Maverick; they both have Starr's best interests at heart. Carlos is put on leave from the police force after he punches the officer who shot Khalil. He lives in a suburb that is wealthier than Garden Heights.

The Hate U Give Glossary

persona

the aspect of someone's character that is presented to or perceived by others

philosophical

relating or devoted to the study of the fundamental nature of knowledge, reality, and existence

morgue

a place where bodies of deceased persons are kept, especially to be identified or claimed

atrium

an open-roofed entrance hall or central court

retaliation

the action of returning a military attack; counterattack

thug

a violent person, especially a criminal

bougie

aspiring to a higher social class. Derived from "bourgeois," or middle/upper class

notorious

famous or well known, typically for some bad quality or deed

rationalize

attempt to explain or justify (one's own or another's behavior or attitude) with logical, plausible reasons, even if these are not true or appropriate

casualty

a person killed or injured in a war or accident

blasphemous

sacrilegious against God or sacred things; profane

grafitti

writing or drawings scribbled, scratched, or sprayed illicitly on a wall or other surface in a public place

radical

a person who advocates thorough or complete political or social reform; a member of a political party or part of a party pursuing such aims

engulf

(of a natural force) sweep over (something) so as to surround or cover it completely

remorse

deep regret or guilt for a wrong committed

douse

pour a liquid over; drench

wrath

extreme anger

increment

an increase or addition, especially one of a series on a fixed scale

activism

the policy or action of using vigorous campaigning to bring about political or social change

piece

a gun, knife, or other weapon

The Hate U Give Themes

Injustice

Khalil's shooting and the ongoing investigation of Officer Cruise put the theme of injustice at the forefront of the novel. The fact that Khalil was unarmed and did not threaten the officer makes his murder unjust. The police are unjust at other points, too, such as when they force Maverick to the ground and pat him down. Race is tied into this theme of injustice as well, since pervasive racism prevents African-Americans from obtaining justice. Starr and Maverick in particular are focused on bringing justice not only for Khalil but also for African-Americans and other oppressed groups, such as the poor. The activist group that Starr joins is called Just Us for Justice because it fights against police maltreatment on the basis of race. At the end of the novel, Starr accepts that injustice might continue but reinforces her determination to fight against it.

Community

The theme of community is significant to the novel, as seen in the way that Garden Heights residents draw together in the face of unspeakable tragedy. At the end of the novel, when Starr and her friends and family work to rebuild Maverick's store, they are supported by cries of encouragement from passerby. This reflects the strong sense of community felt by those who live in Garden Heights, even after their neighborhood has faced physical and emotional destruction. The importance of community is the factor that keeps Maverick tied to the Garden Heights house even though he recognizes that the area is more dangerous than the suburbs. It's evident in the way that Ms. Rosalie's neighbors bring her food when there is no other way they can express their deep sympathy. It's also why Maverick is so determined to help DeVante get out of the gang system, because he knows that the gangs bring about ruptures in the unity of the community.

Race

Race is central to the story that *The Hate U Give* tells. Starr's identity is heavily informed by her race, and Khalil's death is due in part to entrenched racism in the police force. The tension that Starr feels between Garden Heights and Wiliamson Prep is due to differences in wealth and in race. Most of her classmates at school are white, but most of her neighbors are black; Starr feels torn between making sure she's not seen as "too black" at school and making sure she's not "too white" at home. The novel is also undeniably a celebration of blackness. The stereotypes and racism to which African-Americans are subjected is revealed to be extremely pervasive and harmful, even bringing about the death of innocent young men. By dealing directly with the issues of police brutality and protest, the book enters the broader conversation about race relations in America.

Belonging

One of the central issues that Starr faces is a struggle with belonging. From the very beginning of the novel, Starr recognizes that her personality is two-sided. When she's at Williamson, Starr worries that her classmates will think she's "too ghetto." She recognizes that being one of the few black students at the school makes her automatically "cool," but at the same time she censors her own behavior to fit in. Back at home, however—as evidenced by how she feels at Big D's party—people say that Starr thinks she's "all that" and doesn't hang out with them enough, because she attends Williamson. Because of this struggle, Starr is never truly able to be herself in any situation. As the novel progresses, however, Starr learns to embrace both sides of herself, and she brings both sides of her personality together along with friends from both of the spheres of her life.

Bravery

Many people tell Starr that she is brave for speaking up about Khalil, especially when she gives a nationally televised interview. Starr, however, does not share this view. She protests that she isn't brave, that she has been "misdiagnosed" by the people around her who commend her courageousness. It takes Lisa's perspective to point out that bravery is not the same thing as not being afraid. In fact, the very nature of bravery is to act in the face of fear, to refuse to back down even when the task is frightening. By the end of the novel, Starr undeniably demonstrates bravery when she stands on the top of the patrol car to give a speech, lead a chant, and ultimately throw a can of tear gas back at the police. Starr's future in activism will likely be fueled by her continued bravery, which is inspired by the connection she feels with her loved ones both living and dead.

Family

Just as community is an important part of *The Hate U Give*, family is central to the novel as well. The book offers a perspective on nontraditional families and the way these families provide support systems. For example, Starr's family is atypical because Seven doesn't live with the family; he has a different mother than Starr and Sekani. Nevertheless, Maverick and Lisa are able to support Seven in many different ways: they go to his graduation, convince him to go to college outside of the city, talk to him about the importance of not joining a gang, and watch out for him when he goes to the park the day after riots. However, the book explores dysfunctional families as well. King abuses Iesha and his children, and DeVante essentially sacrifices himself in order to remove King from the household, because Iesha is unable or unwilling to stand up to him.

Speaking Up

Starr struggles with speaking up for Khalil for a variety of reasons. She worries that she doesn't deserve to defend Khalil since they had grown far apart in the time before Big D's party. She is also afraid to speak up, and in the midst of trauma and grief, it's difficult for her to take on such an emotionally taxing project as standing up for Khalil in the face of national attention. Kenya inspires Starr to speak up because of her resounding logic: Khalil would have fought for Starr, had she been the one to get shot that night. Maverick also explains that Tupac would have wanted Starr to use her voice, because she can help fight against the oppressive systems that keep minorities from getting ahead. By the end of the book, it's clear that Starr has conquered her fears and recognized the importance of speaking up.

The Hate U Give Quotes and Analysis

"When I was twelve, my parents had two talks with me. One was the usual birds and bees...The other talk was about what to do if a cop stopped me."

Starr, p. 20

This quotation expresses the pervasiveness of police violence and mistreatment of minorities. Even though the national stereotype is that police violence is committed against men, it's evident that brutality at the hands of the police can affect women and girls at well. Furthermore, young age offers no protection from the mistreatment. Starr's parents must talk to Starr about how to behave around police as a minority when she is just twelve years old. They have the talk with Sekani later, even though he is even younger. In addition, Starr's thought process here, as she and Khalil are stopped by the violence, foreshadows the violence that is to follow.

"Fifteen minutes later, I leave the police station with my mom. Both of us know the same thing: This is gonna be some bullshit."

Starr, p. 103

The investigation that Starr participates in does not end up finding fault with Officer Cruise, even though the narrative Starr supplies clearly indicates that Cruise shot at Khalil when he was unarmed and had not threatened Cruise. In addition, the officers ask Starr questions about Khalil's background, such as whether or not he was involved in selling narcotics. At the moment that this question is asked, Starr realizes that the investigation will not be fair or unbiased. Both Lisa and Starr understand that the investigation will fit into a larger narrative of leniency for police violence.

"Ho-ly shit, Starr! Seriously? After everything we've been through, you think I'm a racist? Really?"

Hailey, p. 112

Hailey and Starr's friendship experiences many tensions and ultimately ends, in part because of Hailey's insensitivity toward issues of race. Hailey refuses to grasp that people who are not intentionally racist can still say comments that are in fact racist, or at the very least culturally insensitive. Furthermore, Hailey refuses to engage in conversation with Hailey or Maya about why her remarks were offensive to them. She is blinded towards her own mistakes by defensiveness and a fear of being called a racist. While Maya, for example, listens to Starr and understands why her participation in the Williamson protest was offensive, Hailey refuses to accept Starr's argument and gets angry instead.

"I want my kids to enjoy life! I get it, Maverick, you wanna help your people out. I do too. That's why I bust my butt every day at that clinic. But moving out of the neighborhood won't mean you're not real and it won't mean you can't help this community. You need to figure out what's more important, your family or Garden Heights. I've already made my choice."

Lisa, p. 180

Lisa's argument reflects the internal struggle that both Lisa and Maverick feel about their decision to move out of Garden Heights. On the one hand, they both want to help the other people in their community. Garden Heights is susceptible to poverty and violence, and because Lisa and Maverick have a strong family bond and serve as mentors to young people like DeVante, they want to remain in the neighborhood to continue this assistance. However, they're aware of the dangers of Garden Heights. There are frequent drive-bys, such as the one that killed Natasha. As Lisa points out, it's possible for Maverick to help the community even when he doesn't live there. In addition, moving does not devalue Maverick's commitment to helping others.

"DeVante. Khalil. Neither of them thought they had much of a choice. If I were them, I'm not sure I'd make a much better one."

Starr, p. 239

In the beginning of the novel, Starr was angry at Khalil for choosing to get involved in selling drugs. She didn't understand how he could enable the kind of destructive addiction that affected his mom so much. It takes the perspective of another self-described "thug," DeVante, for Starr to understand what drove Khalil into the dangerous business. He was trying to protect his mother by helping her pay off a debt she had to King after stealing from him. With no other high-paying opportunities available to a young black man living in Garden Heights, Khalil felt forced to turn to drug dealing, just as DeVante felt forced towards the gangs to find a kind of family and sense of community. Here, Starr recounts how talking to Devante helped her realized the dilemma people in his position face, and to understand why they made the choice they did.

"But Ms. Ofrah said this interview is the way I fight. When you fight, you put yourself out there, not caring who you hurt or if you'll get hurt. So I throw one more blow, right at One-Fifteen. 'I'd ask him if he wished he shot me too.'"

Starr, p. 290

Starr's nationally televised interview is a pivotal moment in her transformation from being too afraid and guilty to speak up to Khalil, to leading the protests against his death in the streets of Garden Heights. Starr doesn't condone violent techniques, such as rioting and looting, although she understands the anger that such violence stems from. Instead, as Ms. Ofrah points out, Starr's voice is the most effective weapon she has in fighting injustice. Starr uses the national platform she never wanted or expected to have to speak up not just for Khalil, but for African Americans everywhere.

> "'Y'all gotta come together somehow, man,' Daddy says. 'For the sake of the Garden. The last thing they'd ever expect is some unity around here. A'ight?'"

Maverick, p. 347

Starr realizes the gravity of the moment that Maverick makes this statement. King Lords and Garden Disciples, who are entrenched in a rivalry so deep that it often leads to violence and death, are present in the same room without even a verbal argument breaking out. This is testament to Maverick's powers of farsightedness and communication. But it also demonstrates the seriousness of police brutality. Both Garden Disciples and King Lords are united against the common injustice of racism. While one conversation is certainly not enough to fix the problems that gangs bring to Garden Heights, Maverick's meeting is certainly a step towards unity. He points out that the rivalry between gangs is only detrimental to Garden Heights as a whole.

> "'Everybody wants to talk about how Khalil died,' I say. 'But this isn't about how Khalil died. It's about the fact that he lived. His life mattered. Khalil lived!' I look at the cops again. 'You hear me? Khalil lived!'"

Starr, p. 412

This dramatic moment characterizes Starr's transformation from grieving and afraid to brave activist. Even when she climbs on the police car, Starr is still nervous and unsure if the right words will come to her. In the end, though, Starr simply speaks from the heart, and her impassioned plea for the protestors to focus on Khalil's life rather than his death resonates throughout the crowd. Starr's blog "The Khalil I Know" reflects this principle: that even though Khalil's death was tragic, he should not be seen as a stereotype or a statistic, but as a human being with his own hopes, fears, desires, and goals. Starr directs her statement towards the police officers because she knows that even unconscious dehumanization of African Americans leads to violence and death at the hands of authorities.

> "If I face the truth, as ugly as it is, she's right. I was ashamed of Garden Heights and everything in it. It seems stupid now though. I can't change where I come from or what I've been through, so why should I be ashamed of what makes me, me? That's like being ashamed of myself."

Starr, p. 441

Since she began attending Williamson Prep, Starr has always felt like she lived a double life. There is the "Garden Heights" Starr and the "Williamson Prep" Starr; both of these personas operate on different codes of behavior and use different kinds of language. Kenya has always recognized this duplicity, calling Starr out for pretending to be someone that she really isn't. It takes most of the novel for Starr to come to a similar realization. She accepts that she can't change her experiences, and she questions why she would even want to. Her family, her background, and every event that has occurred in her life have shaped her into the person she now is, so to be ashamed of those events would equate to being ashamed of her very self.

> *"Others are fighting too, even in the Garden, where sometimes it feels like there's not a lot worth fighting for. People are realizing and shouting and marching and demanding. They're not forgetting. I think that's the most important part."*

> *Starr, p. 443*

These powerful lines occur at the end of the novel. They encapsulate the lesson Starr has learned about the importance of speaking up, of using her own voice and perspective to fight for what she believes is right. In addition, this quote points out the importance of not forgetting violence. When deaths such as Khalil's are forgotten, people are not motivated to fight to change the system, and the cycle of violence continues unbroken. Starr also thinks that even when situations seem dire and circumstances appear hopeless, it's essential to have hope and to keep fighting so that a brighter horizon can be created by the very people who are oppressed and their allies.

The Hate U Give Chapters 1 - 3 Summary and Analysis

Summary of Chapters 1 - 3

The novel opens on a spring break party in the gang-contested neighborhood of Garden Heights. 16-year-old Starr Carter feels out of place at the party, which is crowded with dancing teenagers and smells like marijuana. She was pressured to go to the party by Kenya, a girl her age whom she knows because they share an older brother named Seven: Seven's father is Starr's father, and Seven's mother is Kenya's mother. Starr attends Williamson Prep, a school forty-five minutes away from Garden Heights populated by mostly white students; Kenya was able to persuade Starr to attend the party, even though Starr's parents don't allow her to attend parties in the area, because Kenya accused Starr of acting as if she were white. Starr reflects on how she feels out of place both at the spring break party and at Williamson Prep, as Kenya plans to beat up Denasia, a girl at the party she dislikes.

Kenya leaves with two friends to get drinks, and Starr stands alone, feeling awkward. The uncomfortable moment passes when Starr sees Khalil, a close childhood friend. Khalil looks good, and is dressed in fancy clothes and shoes, which makes Starr suspect that he's been making money by selling drugs. Khalil updates Starr on his life—his grandmother lost her job since starting chemotherapy for cancer, and his mother is struggling with a drug habit—and then the two talk and joke together. Suddenly, gunshots ring out from across the room, and partygoers begin scattering.

Khalil grabs Starr's hand and they run to his car. Once inside and driving away from the party, Starr texts Kenya and confirms that she's safe. Starr and Khalil continue to talk as Khalil drives; when Starr asks Khalil whether he's selling drugs, Khalil responds that it's none of her business. The two also reminisce about their childhood. They used to be best friends with another girl named Natasha, who has since passed away. In the middle of their conversation, blue lights flash in the rearview mirror and a siren sounds as a police car pulls Khalil's car over.

Starr remembers that when she was twelve, her parents gave her two talks: one about sex, and one about what to do when interacting with the police. Starr's parents told her not to talk back to the police and to do what they want, so when Khalil "breaks a rule"—asking the officer why he was pulled over instead of taking out his license, registration, and proof of insurance—Starr begins to get nervous. Annoyed that Khalil is talking back, the police officer makes Khalil get out of the car. He pats Khalil down and warns him not to move as he walks back to his patrol car. Khalil opens the driver's door to ask Starr if she's okay, and the police officer shoots him three times in the back. Starr watches with numb horror as blood sprays out of her friend's body and he collapses. She screams in shock and runs to Khalil's body, watching it stiffen as he passes away. The police officer points his gun at her, and she puts her hands up.

People begin to gather around Starr while the police search Khalil's car, then place a sheet over his body. Starr is told to sit in an ambulance as she waits for her parents to arrive. Finally, her father, Maverick, and mother, Lisa, make it to the scene; they sit with Starr and hug her for a long time before driving her home. Still in shock, Starr gets nauseous on the drive home and throws up out the window. Once at home, her mother helps her remove her bloodstained clothes and take a steaming bath. Finally, Starr falls asleep, but nightmares wake her up over and over again.

The next day, Starr wakes up and heads to the kitchen, where her parents and Seven are eating breakfast. Starr lives in her grandmother's old house, which her family inherited after her grandmother moved in with Starr's Uncle Carlos in the suburbs. Seven lives with his father King and King's girlfriend Iesha, as well as Kenya and their sister Lyric. When Starr enters the kitchen, Seven and her father are talking about how King is physically abusive to Iesha, Kenya and Lyric. Seven brings up the elephant in the room—Khalil's death—and the three try to console Starr. They decide not to tell anyone, not even Starr's younger brother Sekani, that Starr was present at the shooting.

To keep Starr busy, her father takes her to the small grocery store that he owns. Starr helps her father sell groceries to the regulars, including Mr. Lewis, a cantankerous old man who angers Starr by being flippant about Khalil's death. Kenya enters the store, and Starr's father gives the girls money to buy lunch at Reuben's, a deli across the street. Kenya asks Starr why she is being so quiet, but Starr doesn't tell her that she saw Khalil get shot. After eating, the two girls walk outside as King, Kenya and Seven's father, pulls up in a BMW. He tries to act familiar with Starr and offers her money for the lunch, but Starr isn't interested; she knows that King is involved in gang business and abusive towards his girlfriend and children. Starr's father approaches the BMW to talk to King. King argues that Starr's father owes him a favor, since he helped him buy his grocery store; but Starr's father points out that since he helped keep King out of prison, the two men are even. He warns King not to touch Seven again, and King drives away angrily.

Analysis of Chapters 1 -3

Starr's discomfort at the party, as well as the fact that she doesn't often spend time with Kenya in social situations, point to the conflict she feels between acting like "Williamson Starr" and "Garden Heights Starr." Williamson Prep is a virtually all-white school, so Starr feels the need to change the way she speaks and acts in order not to be considered "ghetto." Her race already makes her stand out in the homogenous environment, so she changes even small aspects of her personality to fit in at school. Back in her neighborhood, however, the very fact that she attends Williamson Prep makes her an anomaly again. Kenya and others complain that they never see Starr around, and imply that she thinks she's too fancy for the neighborhood.

The fight that occurs at the party reveals the danger of gang presence in Garden Heights. While the violence is senseless, it is also a fact of life for Starr and others who grew up in the neighborhood. Starr, Khalil, and Kenya are upset that the shooting occurred, but not surprised; Kenya even tries to start a fight with a girl as they flee from the party. Gangs, and the violence and drug trade that are inextricably tied up with their existence, are undeniably a part of the social structure of Garden Heights.

Similarly, Khalil's death is shocking in its suddenness, horrifying in its brutality, and tragic in its pointlessness—but it is not entirely unexpected. Starr has known from the age of twelve that many police officers can be expected to treat black people differently than white people. The officer in this case completely fulfills her worst fears. When Khalil doesn't do what the officer tells him to do, the situation quickly escalates into disastrous consequences. His death is a continuation of the theme of meaningless death that Starr has already been exposed to.

Natasha's death represents the ubiquitousness of violence as a result of oppressive social structures and the danger of the gangs in the Garden Heights neighborhood. As a child, Starr had to witness her best friend killed in a drive-by shooting: a senseless killing that takes Natasha as an innocent victim. The experience made Starr aware early on that death and violence are an unfortunate function of the place that she lives in. Starr is no stranger to injustice, and Khalil's death conforms to the narrative of inequity and tragedy that Starr has been forced to be a part of.

Finally, the opening chapters of the book introduce the importance of family to Starr's life. After witnessing an unspeakably horrific act, Starr is comforted by hugs from her parents. The day after the shooting, they are there to help her through the rawness of her pain. Starr's father, Maverick, also defends Seven from King's brutality. Community and family are central to Starr's support system, helping to keep her together in the wake of Khalil's death and offering a positive counterpoint to the cruelty and violence that Starr was drawn into.

The Hate U Give Chapters 4 - 6 Summary and Analysis

Summary of Chapters 4 - 6

In the middle of the night, Starr is awakened by shadowy nightmares about Natasha and Khalil. She starts to walk down the hallway toward the kitchen, and overhears her parents speaking to her mother's brother, Carlos. Carlos lives in a nicer neighborhood than Starr's family and works as a police officer. He tries to convince Starr's parents that Starr should speak to the police about the circumstances of Khalil's shooting as part of an ongoing investigation into the officer's conduct. Starr shifts and the floor creaks, making the adults aware of her presence. Carlos asks her if she would like to speak to the police. Starr is reluctant, but agrees because Carlos promises that it will help Khalil get justice. After Carlos leaves, Starr's father angrily remarks that Carlos was pressuring Starr. Starr thinks that her father doesn't like her uncle because Carlos became Starr's surrogate father from when she was three until she was six, when Maverick spent in prison.

The next morning, Starr and her parents drive to visit Khalil's grandmother, Rosalie. Starr reflects on the fond memories she had playing with Khalil and Natasha at "Ms. Rosalie's" house. The two families are close, since Rosalie took Lisa in after she became pregnant in her senior year of high school and her own mother kicked her out. Rosalie also babysat Starr and Sekani while Lisa finished college.

Lisa knocks, and Tammy—Khalil's aunt—opens the door. The four sit down in the living room with Khalil's younger brother Cameron and Rosalie, who is thinner and wearing a headscarf as she braves the effects of chemotherapy. Rosalie comforts Starr, and tells the group that even though Khalil was involved in selling drugs, he wanted to turn to Maverick for advice on how to get out of the business. Maverick and Lisa give Rosalie money to help pay for the funeral, and the group grieves together.

The next day, Starr's family prays together before Lisa drives Starr and Sekani to school. At school, Starr tries to keep up normal conversation with her friends, but thoughts about Khalil keep intruding. Other problems make Starr uncomfortable at school, too. Her friends enjoyed vacations in the Bahamas and Florida, while Starr's family heads to a local hotel with a swimming pool if they vacation at all. One of Starr's closest friends, Hailey, has been more distant since she unfollowed Starr on Tumblr after Starr reblogged a picture of Emmett Till, a fourteen-year-old black boy murdered for whistling at a white woman in 1955. Starr is also in a fight with her boyfriend, Chris, because Chris pulled out a condom even though Starr had told Chris she wasn't ready for sex. Race further complicates their relationship: although Starr's mother knows she has a white boyfriend, Starr is reluctant to tell her father.

Chris tries to talk to Starr, and starts singing her favorite song—the *Fresh Prince of Bel-Air* theme song. Starr is beginning to lighten up when Chris grabs her hands, and she flashes back to the night Khalil died, thinking of how the cop who shot him was as white as Chris is. She begins to cry and heads into class, leaving Chris confused.

After school, Seven picks up Starr and Sekani and they drive to meet Lisa at the medical clinic where she works. They pick up Chinese food to eat at the clinic. As soon as they sit down to eat, though, they're interrupted by the arrival of Khalil's mother, Brenda. She's not in a good state: her eyes are red from crying, and her body is covered in the sores and scabs indicative of drug abuse. When Starr gets a moment alone with Lisa, she angrily remarks that Brenda has no right to be upset now since she was never a good mother to Khalil. Lisa yells at Starr, arguing that Brenda was Khalil's mother regardless of her mistakes. As Starr brings a plate of food to Brenda and looks in her eyes, she thinks that her mother is right.

At four-thirty, Lisa takes Starr to the police office for the investigation. Two police officers—Detective Gomez, a Latina woman, and Detective Wilkes, a white man—ask Starr about the events surrounding Khalil's shooting. Starr recounts everything that happened, although she can't help but think that Gomez doesn't believe the officer forced Khalil out of the car. Starr begins to get upset and her mother motions for her to leave, but she insists on finishing the interview. She answers a few more questions about how Khalil moved to open the door after the officer left the car, but is blindsided by questions about whether Khalil sold narcotics and if he and Starr had anything to drink at the party. Lisa and Starr leave the station feeling certain that the investigation of the officer who shot Khalil will not be fair.

Analysis of Chapters 4 - 6

Starr's experiences at Williamson point to the difficulty she has in an environment that can often be toxic, because it forces her to pretend to be someone she's not. Starr feels the need to censor herself around her white peers because she doesn't want to be seen only for her race. She is able to fit in and make friends at Williamson, but the barrier of background always separates her from Hailey and Maya, making her hold back fundamental parts of her personality for fear of estranging herself from her wealthier, non-black peers.

This conflict extends to Starr's relationship as well. Starr worries that her father will be angry that she's dating a white boy, because in the past he's viewed black women who date white men negatively. To a large extent, Chris is the white person that Starr can feel most comfortable around. But she never entirely lets her guard down; Chris's wealth and his skin color still stand in the way of complete openness between them. Khalil's shooting further complicates the relationship because it makes Starr more aware than ever of the implications of Chris's whiteness, and the privilege his wealth and skin color have given him to spare him from the challenges Starr has faced.

Khalil's mother, Brenda, serves as an example of the tragic effect drug abuse has had on inner-city communities (as well as suburbs and rural areas) throughout America. Starr is particularly angry that Khalil sold drugs because she saw firsthand the destruction that Brenda's addiction brought upon her family and Khalil himself. Brenda's experience illustrates the tragic circularity of addiction and poverty; Khalil enables other drug users in order to bring his own family out of the circumstances that drug abuse brought upon them. However, Lisa points out that Brenda's addiction does not degrade her as a human being or devalue her emotions.

Starr's experience at the police station advances the theme of the mistreatment of black people at the hands of authorities. The detectives ask about Khalil's character, as if he could be implicated in his own murder because of past experiences that the officer could not have been aware of. Starr feels frustrated in the face of questions that seem to perpetuate a surface representation of Khalil as a drug dealer and a thug—and, by implication, not worthy of life. In the eyes of the police and white America, Khalil's murder is made less impactful and less unjust because of his circumstances in life.

A positive theme explored in these chapters is community. Rosalie supported Lisa and Maverick as they tried to raise a family; Lisa and Maverick pay her back in the form of money, food, and emotional support. The Garden Heights community is beset by violence, but the presence of a strong interconnection between neighbors, friends, and families help provide the solace and comfort necessary to get through the hard times. The juxtaposition of broken and abusive families such as Kenya's alongside loving and supporting families such as Starr's points to the existence of deep problems among the Garden Heights community as well as the existence of care and love.

The Hate U Give Chapters 7 - 9 Summary and Analysis

Summary of Chapters 7 - 9

Starr sits on the bleachers with her friends Hailey and Maya, waiting for gym class to start. With their stomachs full from a fried-chicken cafeteria lunch, they watch as a group of their classmates play a game of girls-vs.-boys basketball. Hailey gets angry that the girls are playing poorly on purpose to flirt with the boys. She convinces Starr and Maya to start their own three-vs.-three game against Chris and two other boys. As they play, Chris asks Starr why she panicked after he touched her the day before, but Starr avoids the question. Chris grabs the ball and makes a run down the court, evading Starr as she tries to catch up with him. Hailey yells at Starr to pretend the ball is some fried chicken if she wants to stay on it.

Starr freezes in anger. She drops the ball and storms off the court to the locker room; Hailey and Maya rush in after her. Hailey insists that she didn't intend the fried chicken comment to be racist, but Starr is unconvinced. Hailey and Maya tell Starr that she's been acting different recently, and ask if she was friends with Khalil. Afraid that Hailey and Maya will treat her differently if they know the truth, Starr denies knowing Khalil. Instead, she lets them believe that she's upset because it's the anniversary of Natasha's death. Her coach lets her go to the office to see the school psychiatrist, but Starr fakes menstrual cramps and calls her Uncle Carlos instead. Carlos takes Starr to a frozen yogurt shop, and they discuss the investigation surrounding Khalil's death. Starr tells Carlos that the officer pointed his gun at her after he shot Khalil, and Carlos hugs Starr as she cries.

The following day is the morning of Khalil's funeral at Christ Temple Church. Starr is disturbed at the sight of Khalil's lifeless body in the coffin, which reminds her of Natasha's similarly cold and inhuman corpse. During the service, her family sits in the front pew, next to Khalil's family. The funeral is framed as a celebration of life rather than a mourning of death, with upbeat songs and prayer. But it takes a more serious turn when April Ofrah, a representative for a Garden Heights-based police accountability advocacy group called Just Us for Justice, takes the podium and tells the funeral-goers that Khalil was unarmed when he was shot. She invites everyone to attend a peaceful protest march after the service.

At the end of Ofrah's speech, King enters the church with Iesha and a group of King Lords. Starr notes that her mother tenses up; she resents Iesha because Maverick got her pregnant with Seven during a "for hire" session he had after a fight with Lisa. King places a folded gray bandana on Khalil's body, which signifies that he was involved with the King Lords. Rosalie angrily throws the bandana back at King, and Maverick convinces him to leave. After the service, Starr cries while her parents comfort her. April Ofrah approaches her and tells her to get in touch when and if she is ready to, because Just Us for Justice wants Starr to tell her side of the story.

That night, riots break out all over Garden Heights. Maverick sleeps at the store to guard it from looters while Lisa, Sekani, Seven, and Starr gather in their den. Machine-gun fire rings out in the neighborhood, and TV footage shows police cars set ablaze. Starr has trouble falling asleep, and when she finally does, nightmares jolt her back awake. It is morning, and Seven is banging on her door, asking Starr to go to the park with him for basketball like they usually do on the last Saturday of the month. Although Starr is reluctant to leave because of last night's violence, she agrees and yells to her parents to let them know where she's going.

Seven and Starr play basketball at Rose Park. Seven is unathletic, and Starr easily beats him, but the two enjoy their game until two men wearing Celtics jerseys approach them. These are Garden Disciples, and they harass Seven because he lives with King, a King Lord—pulling a knife and asking Seven to give them his phone and sneakers. DeVante, a younger King Lord who was posted in the park to sell drugs, approaches the Garden Disciples and reminds them that Rose Park is King Lord territory, showing them his gun. After the Garden Disciples leave, Seven thanks DeVante and offers his condolences for his brother, Dalvin, who died last week.

Maverick pulls up in a white Tahoe and yells at Starr and Seven for leaving the house the night after riots without telling him (neither he nor Lisa heard Starr's shout on her way out). Back at home, Lisa and Maverick angrily declare that Starr is grounded, taking away her cell phone. Lisa takes Sekani and Starr to Carlos's house for the day. On the way there, they see protestors, and Starr feels like the riots are her fault because she was unable to convince the police that the officer who shot Khalil should be arrested.

At Carlos's house, Carlos's wife Pam cooks meat on the grill while their young children, Daniel and Ava, play in the backyard. Starr's grandmother, who lives with Carlos, complains to Lisa that Pam has been taking her food and cooking it the wrong way. The doorbell rings, and when Starr opens the door she finds Chris, who lives down the street from Carlos and saw Starr's family drive past. He asks Starr why she's been upset recently, and Starr admits that she feels distant from him because he is white and rich, and she is not. Chris reassures her that they can make the relationship work despite their differences. Starr feels encouraged that Chris truly cares for her, and she decides to make up with him, taking his hand and leading him to the backyard for dinner.

Analysis of Chapters 7 - 9

Hailey's fried-chicken insult explores a complication of racism: the fact that, as Starr points out, people who are not intentionally racist can still say racist things. This is especially possible in an environment like Williamson, where the student body is virtually all white and students might not even be aware that their comments are hurtful and prejudiced. Instead of listening to Starr, Hailey gets upset and offended that Starr has accused her of making a thoughtless remark. This represents a difficulty often found in the conversation of race in America: defensiveness which prevents open communication.

Starr and Carlos's relationship further explores the theme of family. Many of the families in the book are non-conventional, but are still able to offer strong support systems for their members. In this case, Carlos and Maverick compete because Maverick feels that Carlos replaced him as a father figure during Starr's formative years. While both Carlos and Maverick care deeply for Starr, their feelings of pride get in the way of their relationship with her and with each other. Starr resents the fact that two people who care for each other constantly fight; ironically, they fight because they both believe they have her best interests at heart.

The importance of gangs to life in Garden Heights is made more evident by these chapters. The strict division of men into King Lords and Garden Disciples structures every aspect of life in the neighborhood, including even funerals. King's placement of the bandana on Khalil's body is an attempt to use Khalil to represent his gang even after he has died. When Starr and Seven encounter conflict in Rose Park, the possibility of violence that hinges on every interaction between gang members is made alarmingly evident. Residents of Garden Heights have to be on their toes and armed in order to deal with the potential violence that is tied up in the operation of gangs.

In addition, these chapters explore a controversial issue in American current events: violent protests in response to police mistreatment of African Americans. Garden Heights residents are passionately angry about the constant oppression of their friends, families, neighbors, and themselves; some react violently, and protests lead to riots and to looting. These forms of protest contrast with the peaceful march organized by Just Us for Justice, and they also speak to the larger ideology conflict between people like Maverick, who espouse the ideology of the Black Panthers, and people like Mr. Lewis, who argues for Dr. King's ideology.

Finally, Starr and Chris's relationship is made more difficult by the differences between them: they live in different places, come from different backgrounds, and have different skin colors. Starr worries that their differences will make it hard for the relationship to work because they put distance between the two. Chris has more optimism about the ability of their relationship to work despite the undeniably different ways they experience the world. Uncle Carlos's house provides a physical space for Starr's "Garden Heights" and "Williamson" worlds to mix, just as Starr feels that to some extent she can combine her two selves when she is with Chris.

The Hate U Give Chapters 10 - 12 Summary and Analysis

Summary of Chapters 10 - 12

Starr, Lisa, and Sekani spend the night at Carlos's house, because riots begin again at sundown in Garden Heights. On their way back the next morning, a police roadblock slows traffic, and Starr has to close her eyes to stop herself from panicking when the police ask her mother for ID and proof of insurance. Back at home, Starr's father has to go the warehouse for the store. He takes Starr along with him, promising to buy her ice cream, and the two talk about Tupac's philosophy on Thug Life. Starr's father explains that an oppressive system keeps minorities stuck in poverty and forces them to sell drugs to stay afloat. They come to the conclusion that Starr can't stay silent in the face of the Khalil's murder.

Maverick and Starr head to the store. While Starr works affixing stickers to snack bags, there's a knock at the door, and DeVante enters. He looks nervous and wanders around the store, refusing to leave even after Maverick gives him an ultimatum. They question him and find out that he's hiding from King. DeVante asks Maverick how he was able to get out of the King Lords. Maverick explains that his father, Adonis Carter, was one of the city's biggest drug dealers. Maverick grew up wealthy, but his father went to prison when he was eight, and Maverick became a King Lord at twelve. After he became a father, Maverick wanted to leave the game, but he was making money and couldn't figure out how to get out. Finally, when he and King were busted by the police, he took the charge and went to prison for three years. King let him leave the King Lords after this, because of the debt he owed him. At the end of his story, Maverick agrees to help DeVante leave the King Lords, and offers him a job at the store. He also agrees for DeVante to move in with the family; later that night, Starr hears her parents arguing about this decision and whether or not the family should move out of Garden Heights.

At school on Monday morning, Starr immediately notices that the halls are quieter than usual. She finds out from her friends that Hailey's older brother Remy is organizing a protest about Khalil—not because of solidarity for his death, but because they want to get out of class. Starr angrily lashes out at her friends for exploiting Khalil's death. She refuses to take part in the protest; a few other students, including Chris and her friend Jess, sit out as well.

Seven picks Sekani and Starr up after school, and the three head to the store. There's a TV crew on the street, filming Mr. Lewis, who owns a shop near the grocery store. Mr. Lewis tells the cameraman that he saw King Lords jump police officers nearby. He even mentions King by name. After the interview, Maverick warns Mr. Lewis that his life will be in serious danger after the King Lords see the broadcast. Mr.

Lewis insists that he's not afraid after fighting a war and getting stabbed by white segregationists.

Suddenly, a police car stops near Mr. Lewis and Maverick, and an officer asks the two men if there's a problem. They insist that they're just talking, but the officer becomes violent, forcing Maverick to get on the ground with his hands behind his back. The officer keeps his knee on Maverick's back as he pats him down three times, then finally lets him get up. Before leaving, he calls Maverick "boy" and warns him that he's keeping an eye on him.

Back in the store, Maverick pounds the desk with rage. Mr. Reuben's nephew, Tim, makes the situation worse by revealing that some neighborhood people saw Maverick, Lisa, and Starr leave the crime scene on the night of Khalil's death, so they suspect that Starr is the witness whose testimony failed to get the officer arrested. Kenya, who is in the store to buy groceries for her family, overhears Tim. She accuses Starr of being a coward for not publicly defending Khalil. Starr tells Maverick, and he promises that he will back her up if and when she decides to speak out.

Back at home, Maverick is weeding when Starr sees a tank roll down the street. A uniformed officer holds a rifle on top of the tank, warning the neighborhood that anyone violating the 10 p.m. curfew will be arrested. Starr and Maverick head inside; Lisa has bought pizza for dinner. Starr eats pizza while working on her new Tumblr, an anonymous blog called "The Khalil I Know" where she posts childhood pictures of Khalil along with facts about him that present a fuller picture of his personality.

Starr's mother lets her take the next day off of school. The defense attorney wants to speak to Starr, so her parents take her to Ms. Ofrah of Just Us for Justice. Ofrah explains that the case will be taken to a grand jury, and that the gun the officer thought Khalil had was actually a hairbrush. She offers to represent Starr pro bono in the upcoming case. Starr accepts, and agrees to a television interview, with Maverick's stipulation that her identity be protected. Before the conversation can continue, Maverick gets a call from DeVante; something has happened at the store, and he needs help.

Analysis of Chapters 10 - 12

Tupac Shakur was an American actor and rapper whose rap lyrics frequently centered around the hardship of inner-city life, racism, and social oppression. The acronym Shakur created for "Thug Life"—The Hate U Give Little Infants Fucks Everybody—is an important motif in the novel that also provides the title of the book. Starr and Maverick's discussion of the meaning of "Thug Life" offers insight into their respective philosophies about what the acronym might refer to.

Khalil said that "Thug Life" refers to how the hate that society feeds its youth comes back to bite them later; Starr generalizes this to the hate that black people, minorities, poor people, and the oppressed are forced to deal with. Maverick extends Starr's point further, explaining that so many people in Garden Heights are drug dealers because they have a lack of educational and career opportunities. The conversation is important because it further opens Starr's eyes to the injustice all around her and makes her more determined to speak up for Khalil.

Maverick's explanation of the cyclical gang violence in Garden Heights is further reinforced by DeVante's experience. He joined the King Lords to provide for himself and his brother, but the violence he experienced makes him want to get out of the game. He turns to Maverick for advice, but Maverick explains how difficult it is for a person to extricate themselves from the intensely loyal groups; Maverick himself had to go to prison in order to be able to safely leave the King Lords. DeVante's experience makes it evident that in order to leave a gang, it's important to have an external support system (such as the one that Maverick, Lisa, and Carlos are able to provide him with).

The theme of police mistreatment of minorities is further explored in these chapters. Even though Maverick and Mr. Lewis are simply having a verbal disagreement, the police officer who sees them talking responds with an incredibly disproportionate display of violence—especially after he determines that Maverick is Starr's father. The way he forces Maverick to the ground and pats him down three times illustrates the inherent distrust that he has of Maverick because of his appearance—especially his skin color. It's this distrust that leads to extreme mistreatment such as Khalil's shooting.

Finally, Starr's blog offers an important perspective on Khalil after he has been dismissed as a drug dealer and thug by the general public. Her tender snapshots of Khalil's life demonstrate the importance of not limiting people to stereotypes, or subconsciously assuming that their lives are worth less than others because of the background they come from. It's also a first step in the direction of speaking up, demonstrating Starr's bravery and determination to do something even though she is deeply afraid of the consequences of doing so. Starr uses the public, technological platform of Tumblr to transmit a better and more complete image of Khalil to a broad audience.

The Hate U Give Chapters 13 - 15 Summary and Analysis

Summary of Chapters 13 - 15

Mr. Lewis has been beaten up by a group of King Lords. At first, Maverick thinks that the King Lords were angry about Mr. Lewis's TV interview; but Mr. Lewis tells him that the gang was looking for DeVante, since he stole $5,000 from King. Maverick decides to take DeVante to the safety of Carlos's house, and the family drives over. Starr is upset to find out that Carlos was put on leave from the police force; she blames herself. Carlos agrees to let DeVante stay with him and help him through online school, although Starr's grandmother disapproves.

As Carlos begins to tell DeVante about the rules of living in his house, Chris rings the doorbell. He saw the family's car and wanted to check on Starr because she missed school that day. Starr tells Maverick that Chris is her boyfriend, and he reacts angrily because Chris is white—and because, apparently, Carlos already knew. DeVante also makes a disparaging remark to Starr because he thinks Chris is trying to act black. Chris and Starr sit at the counter talking; they start kissing, and Lisa walks in, embarrassing them. Starr asks her mother about the fight she had with Maverick over moving out of Garden Heights.

DeVante and Starr sit at the kitchen table eating graham crackers and talking about Khalil. DeVante tells Starr that Khalil wasn't a King Lord—he turned King down, so King put a gray bandana on his body in an attempt to save face—and that the reason Khalil sold drugs was to repay his mother's debt after she stole money from King. DeVante explains that he and his brother joined the King Lords for the financial support and the chance to be cared for.

Starr leaves Carlos's and walks to Maya's house. She finds Hailey and Maya playing a video game in Maya's bedroom, and although she joins them, awkwardness hangs over the room. Hailey acknowledges the tension, and Starr admits that she's angry at Maya and Hailey for taking part in the disingenuous protest. Maya apologizes, but Hailey refuses, and insists that Starr apologize for accusing her of being racist.

The three turn back to the TV. An interview with the father of Brian Cruise, Jr.—the officer who shot Khalil—is playing on a news station. Cruise's father insists that Khalil was speeding and threatened his son. He also says that Cruise was physically attacked by a fellow officer, which Starr realizes must be Carlos. After the interview, Hailey says that she feels bad for Cruise's family, since his life matters too. Starr angrily replies that his life always matters more. Starr asks Hailey why she unfollowed her Tumblr; Hailey responds that it's because she doesn't know who Starr is anymore, and storms out.

Maya tells Starr that Hailey was lying—she unfollowed Starr's Tumblr because she didn't want to see pictures relating to black power. Maya, who is Chinese, also reveals that Hailey once asked her if her family ate a cat for Thanksgiving; Maya had laughed because she felt uncomfortable, and Starr had laughed too. Starr and Maya agree not to let Hailey get away with making more racist comments.

After hanging out with Maya, Starr walks back to Carlos's. She's surprised to find him drinking a beer; he doesn't drink because his and Lisa's mother is an alcoholic and was abusive to her kids. Carlos admits that he punched Officer Cruise because he was angry that Cruise had pointed his gun at Starr. He also tells Starr that he was sure that he wouldn't have killed Khalil had he been in Cruise's position.

On the morning of the day Starr has to talk to the DA, Lisa takes her to IHOP for breakfast. Lisa notices that Starr isn't eating and asks her what's wrong, and Starr tells her about her fight with Hailey. They head back to Garden Heights so Starr can change into nicer clothes. At the house, they find that Maverick has burnt breakfast; he and Lisa bicker.

Maverick and Lisa take Starr to the office of Karen Monroe, the DA. Starr answers her questions about the events surrounding Khalil's death, but when it's time to recount the actual shooting, she gets sick and begins vomiting. As her parents help her back to the car, Starr resents that she can feel others pitying her.

Maverick takes Starr to the store for the rest of the day. He admits that he was upset Starr was dating a white boy because he thought it meant that he hadn't set a good example of a black man, but Starr reassures him that he has set a good example of a man regardless of race. Suddenly, a gray BMW pulls up, and King approaches Maverick to ask where DeVante is. Maverick insists that he doesn't know, and King threatens him that Starr better not implicate the King Lords from her platform as the witness of Khalil's death.

Maverick is shaken afterward, and he closes the store early. He and Starr pick up dinner from Reuben's on the way home. At dinner, Lisa reveals some good news: she has an interview for the Pediatrics Nursing Manager position at Markham Memorial Hospital—a high-paying position. Maverick agrees to move out of Garden Heights. However, Seven insists that he won't go to a college away from home because he wants to protect his sisters, who are frequently subjected to King's abuse.

Analysis of Chapters 13 - 15

Maverick's reaction to Chris represents a racialized attitude toward romantic relationships. It's reflective of a cultural norm that dictates same-race relationships for many different races. As a protective father figure, Maverick is naturally wary of any boy that Starr chooses to date, and the fact that Chris is white further complicates this protectiveness. Maverick's attitude toward famous women of color who date white men already made Starr nervous about telling her father about her relationship.

The interview with Officer Cruise's father is understandably frustrating for Starr to watch. It's a defensive interview that is full of untruths. While Cruise is trying to protect his son from the court of public opinion, Starr's knowledge of the events as they actually occurred contrasts sharply with the narrative that Cruise reports. Even more difficult for Starr to hear is Hailey's reaction, which typifies the reaction of a white perspective on police violence.

Both before and after commenting on the interview, Hailey continues to exhibit a casual racism towards both Starr and Maya. Her attitude is entirely unapologetic; she refuses even to engage in conversation with her friends about why her comments might be offensive to them. This closed-mindedness reflects a larger difficulty of having a productive conversation about race in America.

Because feelings of shame and defensiveness are tied up with white privilege, Hailey doesn't want to acknowledge that her viewpoints are upsetting to her non-white friends. Furthermore, Hailey seems to firmly believe that she is not being racist. Despite her good intentions, she makes offensive remarks—and then refuses to listen to Starr and Maya's side of the story.

Starr and her family also struggle with the decision of whether or not to move out of Garden Heights. There are several components to the decision: the need to stay safe, the ability to afford a larger house, the desire to help others in Garden Heights, and the pull of a place that has always been home. The decision of whether or not to stay is a significant source of tension between Maverick and Lisa. Both want to provide community and assistance to their neighbors, and to avoid being seen as sell-outs; however, Lisa is determined to move because she wants her children to be in a safer environment.

The Hate U Give Chapters 16 - 18 Summary and Analysis

Summary of Chapters 16 - 18

Ms. Ofrah arranges for Starr to do an interview with a national news program, one week before she will testify in front of the grand jury. She helps Starr prepare for a week in advance; after practicing, Starr helps out at Just Us for Justice. On the way to the interview, Starr gets a text from Chris about the prom next Saturday; Chris and DeVante are becoming friends.

The interviewer, Diane Carey, asks Starr who Khalil was to her, and Starr replies that he was a jokester with a big heart—a kid. She says that Officer Cruise pointed his gun at her, and she reveals why Khalil sold drugs, but points out that even if he had been in a gang it wouldn't have justified his shooting. Finally, Carey asks her what she would say to Officer Cruise if he was sitting here. Starr says that she would ask him if he wished he shot her too.

Starr's interview is an instant hit; by the next morning, it's one of the most-watched interviews in the network's history. An anonymous donor offers to pay for Starr's college tuition, and she receives a flood of emails and texts supporting her, including one from Kenya. She also receives death threats, however, and a warning from King.

That Saturday, Starr goes to the prom with Chris, but he's acting distant. She and Maya dance together while Hailey continues to give them the cold shoulder. Finally, Chris yells at Starr after asking if she wants a picture together. Starr runs to hide in the Rolls-Royce that Chris hired to drive them. He climbs inside the car, and tells Starr that he knows she's the witness of Khalil's death and is upset that she hid it from him.

Starr explains that she liked that Chris could let her retain normality in her life and was afraid that he would see her as just the girl from the hood. Chris reassures Starr that he won't judge her, and Starr tells him about Natasha's death and the difficulty of growing up in poverty. Chris embraces Starr and the two say "I love you" for the first time. They go back to the dance; Starr thinks that the night is one of the best of her life.

The next day, Starr's family drives to the suburbs to check out the house that Maverick and Lisa plan on buying. Maverick confronts Seven about his plan to attend community college, and convinces him to go to college away from home because it offers more opportunities. The family prays together, and Lisa thanks her mother for giving her money for the down payment.

Back in Garden Heights, Starr's family watches a basketball game together in the den. In the middle of the game, gunshots ring out and bullets fly through a front window. Maverick runs to the door and shoots at a receding group of men right after someone throws a brick through the living room window. No one is hurt, but Carlos comes over to survey the damage. He and Maverick debate whether the perpetrators are King Lords or police looking to scare Starr on the night before she will testify to the grand jury. Starr insists that she won't testify because she doesn't want to endanger the family; Maverick responds by invoking the anti-oppression ideologies of Malcolm X and the Black Panthers. Carlos gets angry when he finds out that Maverick called two Cedar Grove King Lords to guard the house for the night.

Analysis of Chapters 16 - 18

The mixed reactions to Starr's interview characterize the highly polarized environment surrounding the discussion of race and police brutality in America today. While many applaud Starr's bravery and appreciate her perspective, others respond with death threats or simple indifference. As much as Starr attempts to defend Khalil and point out that his life decisions didn't affect the events surrounding his death, it's clear that some people dismiss both Starr and Khalil by virtue of their backgrounds and their skin color.

Likewise, the difficulty Star experiences in allowing Chris to see all sides of her life reflects her worry that he will dismiss her as "ghetto." Even though Khalil and Natasha's deaths were such significant events in her life, Starr is reluctant to tell Chris about it, in part because she feels that his life has been so different from hers that he would be unable to understand the pain she's gone through. Chris offers a different perspective: even though he and Starr are separated by their past experiences, they can still open up to each other, love each other, and accept each other.

Seven's conflict over whether or not he should leave for college is similar to Maverick's inner turmoil about the decision to leave Garden Heights. Both Seven and Maverick want what is best for their families. Seven wants to protect his mother and sisters from King's abuse; Maverick points out that it should be the role of a parent to care for their child, not vice versa. The decision is made more complicated by the fact that colleges located further away can offer better opportunities for Seven than the community college. Seven's ultimate decision to accept Maverick's advice and attend a different college reflects his determination to further his position in life and improve himself, but he still experiences conflict because he wants the best for those he loves.

In these chapters, readers can see Starr's continued struggle as she is torn between the need to speak and the urge to keep quiet. The nature of this fear has changed as well. Earlier, Starr was reluctant to speak up because she wasn't yet ready, still reeling from the aftermath of Khalil's death and unsure if she could even help bring him to justice. After unknown assailants throw a brick through her window, however,

Starr's reluctance to use her voice on a national platform is related more towards fear that she will endanger her family than to personal fears about her own readiness for the challenge. It takes Maverick's Black Panther-based arguments to reorient her towards speaking up in the face of potential danger.

The Cedar Grove King Lord's act of protection for Starr and her family adds to the narrative that gang members cannot be written off as thugs or criminals. Khalil and DeVante's situations demonstrate how a lack of opportunities for poor, young black men can drive them towards the streets as a means of gaining subsistence and a surrogate family. While involvement in gangs often leads toward imprisonment or death, many—such as DeVante and Khalil—feel as if they have no other choice. In this way, the novel works to challenge preconceived views of of gang members and offers insight into why street violence occurs.

The Hate U Give Chapters 19 - 21 Summary and Analysis

Starr wakes up on the day of the grand jury to find her kitchen filled with Cedar Grove King Lords. She brings a plate of food out to Maverick and Carlos, who are sitting in the back of Maverick's Tahoe. The two men have talked to each and made up for Starr's sake.

The King Lords drive with Starr and her family to the courthouse. Not only is Starr nervous about the trial, but the courthouse also brings back memories of her father's conviction and imprisonment. Starr's parents comfort her in the moments before she has to enter the jury room, reassuring her that she is brave for doing exactly what she's afraid of. In the grand jury, the DA questions Starr about the night of the events. Starr finds the experience painful, but knows that she has to do what she can to bring Khalil justice.

Chapter 20 is set eight weeks after Khalil's death. It's been two weeks since Starr talked to the grand jury, and she and her family and community are on edge. At school, Hailey confronts Starr with a picture from her twelfth birthday party: Khalil is in the shot, meaning that Starr lied to Hailey about knowing him. Maya and Starr try to get Hailey to apologize for her racist comments, but she refuses, going as far as to say that the officer did everyone a favor by killing a drug dealer.

Starr loses her temper and attacks Hailey, punching and kicking her. Hailey fights back, and when Hailey's older brother Remy calls Starr a crazy bitch, Seven appears and pushes Remy away. Two security guards break up the fight, and all four are suspended for three days. Lisa picks up Starr and Seven and takes them home; Starr has an outburst of rage in the car, pounding the dashboard in frustration over the pain that Khalil's death has brought her.

Back at home, Lisa, Starr, and Seven find Maverick talking to a group of King Lords and Garden Disciples in the kitchen. He points out that even if the jury fails to indict Officer Cruise, the gangs have to stop riots from occurring again because they get out of hand and hurt the black community. Maverick even gets Goon, a King Lord, to shake hands with a Garden Disciple, marking the beginning of a form of unity in Garden Heights. He and Lisa decide not to punish Seven and Starr for the fight, knowing that they probably would have lashed out themselves if they were in their children's place.

Chapter 21 takes place two weeks later, on a Saturday. Starr's family, her friends, and Seven's friends are all at Carlos's house for Seven's birthday party, which doubles as a graduation party since he graduated from high school on Friday. Starr is nervous about whether she should act "white" or "black" since DeVante, Kenya, Maya, and Chris are all at the party, but is relieved when the five have a warm, joking conversation.

Starr's family leads a group dance party. Eventually, Starr heads inside to get something to eat, but the phone starts ringing—Iesha is at the gate, wanting to be let in. Seven, Kenya, Starr, Lisa, and Maverick walk to meet her. Iesha confronts Seven about not inviting her to the party, but Seven angrily replies that Iesha has been a bad mother to him, not even bothering to show up to his graduation. He accuses Iesha of never loving him the way that he loved her. Before driving away, an irate Iesha warns Maverick that King will hurt his family because Starr implicated him during her interview.

Back inside, Kenya apologizes to Starr for Iesha's threat. Starr says that she emphasizes with Iesha, knowing from her fear of speaking up about Khalil that it can be difficult to stand up for oneself. She tells Kenya to encourage Iesha to take a stand, but Kenya is doubtful. The two girls head to the backyard, where Maverick and Lisa present Seven with a cake. The group sings happy birthday, eats cake, and spends the rest of the night dancing and laughing together.

Analysis of Chapters 19 - 21

Starr's fear of the courthouse reflects the cyclical nature of imprisonment brought about by violence and poverty in the face of an oppressive social and criminal justice system. Maverick was in prison at the same time that his father was; both men were pulled into the nebulous world of street gangs. In fact, Maverick was essentially jailed because of his father—he became a King Lord at twelve, following in the footsteps of his big-time gangster father. Maverick's sacrifice for King enabled him to leave the King Lords; the fact that he had to take prison time to leave the game demonstrates the difficulty of breaking a negative cycle.

The fight that Starr has with Hailey brings out an interesting new aspect of her character. Starr points out that a stage of grief is anger, and she has much to be angry about, from Khalil's death to her friend's unapologetic racism. The fact that this anger actually translates into violence points to how deeply rooted it is. Starr lashes out because she is angry at recent events, and because of the steadily building tensions of feeling forced to hide important parts of herself at Williamson. The racism and hate that imbues Starr's environment pushes her to the breaking point, and her internal anger bubbles over into physical action.

Maverick's ability to bring the King Lords and Garden Disciples together is a pivotal moment in the narrative of gang violence and rivalry explored thus far in the book. Although he is by no means able to end the turf wars that plague Garden Heights, Maverick nonetheless makes the gang members understand that they are united against a common enemy—race-based mistreatment in the police force and in society as a whole. The meeting in Maverick's kitchen is an optimistic moment in the midst of turmoil and sadness.

Seven's party gives Starr the chance to combine her two separate worlds for the first time. She's incredibly apprehensive about the moment that her Williamson friends meet her Garden Heights friends, and she's not sure how to act—what kind of words and expressions should she use? How should she conduct herself? The fact that Starr is able to relax and be her authentic self is testament to the open-mindedness of her friends as well as the essential fact that people are more similar than different. Just because her two spheres of existence involve different experiences and norms of behavior doesn't mean that they can't coexist in the neutral space of Carlos's house.

The relationship between Iesha and Seven is a heartbreaking example of how the bonds of family unity can strain in the face of abuse and hardship. Although Seven always tried to protect his mother, he feels that she never reciprocated his love. It's especially painful that Iesha didn't show up to his graduation, because this was a proud and significant moment in his life. Still, Iesha feels the bonds of motherhood connecting her to her son, and she is hurt and angry when she sees the distance that exists between them. She is clearly misguided, but as Starr points out, it can be extremely difficult to find a way to navigate life when trapped in a terrifying situation of abuse.

The Hate U Give Chapters 22 - 24 Summary and Analysis

Chapter 22 takes place thirteen weeks after Khalil's death. Starr's family has moved into their new house in the suburbs, but to Starr it doesn't feel like home yet. The grand jury is due to announce their decision in a few hours; feeling nervous, Starr calls Chris. The two hang out in Chris's bedroom, and Starr tells Chris that they shouldn't be together because of the difference in their races, backgrounds, and wealth. Chris reassures her that they should be together. When Starr tries to initiate sex, he tells her that it's not a good time because she's not in a good emotional place. Starr cries into his chest, and they fall asleep.

Starr wakes up a few hours later to a frantic call from Seven: Lisa and Carlos are out looking for Starr, and DeVante has been hurt. Seven picks Starr and Chris up, and they drive to King's house. They find DeVante and Kenya in Iesha's bedroom; DeVante is bruised and bloody because some King Lords jumped him while he was visiting his brother's grave. King and his gang party in the backyard, waiting until sundown to kill DeVante.

Iesha walks into her bedroom and threatens to let King know that Seven is there. Ultimately, she tells Seven to take Kenya, Lyric, and DeVante and leave the house—an act of sacrifice, since King will undoubtedly take his anger out on Iesha once he finds out that DeVante is gone. Seven is angry at first that Iesha told him to leave so she could party, but Starr points out that she was trying to help. Seven turns the car around, wanting to protect Iesha from King, but the others convince him to accept his mother's attempt to save him. As he turns the car once again, a radio program announces that the grand jury decided not to indict Officer Cruise.

The group sits in stunned silence as Seven drives them to his grandmother's house. Starr gets angry that, after all her efforts, she was unable to get justice for Khalil. She decides that she wants to protest and riot—since the police don't care about her, she doesn't care about the police. Kenya takes Lyric into her grandmother's house in case Iesha shows up, while Seven, Chris, DeVante, and Starr drive to Magnolia where protests are occurring.

They park and walk onto the street, where King Lords and Garden Disciples burn a police car together, then move onto burning and looting all the stores on the street that aren't tagged with "Black owned" graffiti. Groups of people chant "Fuck the police!" to an NWA song playing on a speaker, while a line of police in riot gear march down the street, followed by tanks. As more explosions occur and smoke fills the street, Starr and her friends rush back to Seven's car and drive away.

Back in the car, conversation turns to the differences between black and white people. Seven points out that Chris has fallen into the trap of the white standard when Chris asks why black people have "odd" names. The group decides to go help

Maverick protect the store, but there are so many roadblocks that they are forced to go to the east side—Garden Disciples territory. Seven's car runs out of gas, and they are forced to abandon it to walk down the street to a gas station.

On their way to the gas station, the group runs into more protests occurring on Carnation, the street where Khalil was shot. Starr sees Ms. Ofrah leading protest chants from the top of a patrol car. Ms. Ofrah is surprised to Starr out on the street. When Starr explains that she's fed up and wants to protest, Ms. Ofrah asks Starr to fire her so if her parents find out that she helped Starr protest, she wasn't acting as her attorney but as an activist. Then she hands Starr a bullhorn.

From the top of the police car, Starr speaks passionately to the crowd about the wrongness of Khalil's death. She leads a chant, "Khalil lived!" before the police throw a can of tear gas at her. She picks up the can and hurls it back towards the police; chaos breaks out on the street. Stumbling and choking on tear gas, Starr, Seven, DeVante, and Chris are saved by Goon, the Cedar Grove King Lord who is a friend of Maverick's. Goon lets them into his pickup truck and drives them to the store.

Protected by its "black owned" graffiti tag and boarded windows, the store has not been ruined by the riots. Once inside, Goon and those who were riding in his truck—including a national news anchor—grab milk from the aisles and pour it over their faces to alleviate the burning feeling in their eyes.

Starr checks her phone and realizes that her mother has left her increasingly irate voicemails; she saw Starr's speech at the protest on TV. Seven and Starr reluctantly head to the store's office to call Lisa back, knowing that she will be furious. Suddenly, a glass bottle with a flaming cloth tucked in the mouth soars through the window, and the store explodes.

Analysis of Chapters 22 - 24

The tender moment between Starr and Chris, where Starr finally seems to begin accepting that they should be together despite the vast differences in their upbringings, is an optimistic break before the waves of racial turmoil and anger that follow in the rest of this section. Although the jury fails to indict Officer Cruise, sparking widespread anger over this reinforcement of racism, Starr and Chris are one example of how differences in background can be overcome. Their relationship makes it clear that the practice of communication and acceptance would do well to help reduce "isms" in society.

Starr and the African-American Garden Heights community are deeply wounded by the fact that Khalil will not get justice for being shot while unarmed. However, Starr and her friends are not surprised by the decision. They are already accustomed to systemic racism and aware of the results of many grand jury decisions over police violence cases across the United States. The fact that Khalil is not indicted contributes to a theme of the book, that protest and the struggle for ultimate good is more important than isolated failures; rather than becoming entirely discouraged, Starr is still determined to fight for African-American rights.

This section also offers insight into the reasons that rioting and looting tend to follow jury decisions of this magnitude. While Starr had always steered clear of the riots before, she adopts the attitude that if the police don't seem to care about African Americans, then she won't care about the police. This is a continuation of the overwhelming anger that Starr felt when she fought Hailey. The discontent is so great that it can't be contained without physical expression; Starr feels the need to do something even though the atmosphere is dangerous.

The conversation between Starr, DeVante, Seven, and Chris brings up an interesting exploration of the white standard. While Chris is not intentionally racist, he still exhibits a bias toward white cultural norms by referring to African-American names as odd or unusual. This conversation also offers a playful examination of what makes a person white or black. By "testing" Chris with examples of black culture, Starr, DeVante, and Seven push up against the question of what defines that culture.

Finally, a pivotal moment in the novel comes when Starr stands on the police car to speak. We have now seen a major transformation from when she was first afraid to let her voice to be heard: thirteen weeks later, she is yelling into a megaphone before a full crowd and throwing a can of tear gas back at the police. Kenya's pointed advice to Starr not to be silent is fully realized in her brave stand at the protest on Carnation Street. Even though the jury failed to indict Officer Cruise, Starr is not cowed but determined to continue to stand up for justice.

The Hate U Give Chapters 25 & 26 Summary and Analysis

Summary of Chapters 25 & 26

Flames tear down the store's aisles. Seven, Chris, DeVante, and Starr rush towards the back door, but the burglar bars prevent them from getting out, and the keys are by the front of the store where the fire is. They yell for help, and Tim Reubens, who was outside protecting his uncle's deli, rushes to the back of the store and begins beating on the door. A few moments later, Maverick runs up as well and unlocks the door.

Everyone gets out just as the store is enveloped in flames. As they sit with Maverick, Lisa, and Carlos on the curb outside, trying to catch their breath, they notice King and a group of King Lords sitting on the hood of a gray BMW parked in the intersection. King is laughing and pointing. Maverick confronts him, and Carlos has to hold Lisa back from doing the same. Before anything can happen, however, police cars and fire trucks arrive.

Mr. Lewis tells the police that King started the fire, but since he didn't see it happen, the police don't believe him. Then Maverick breaks precedent by snitching and telling the cops that he saw King start the fire. Mr. Reuben, Tim, and others who have gathered on the street to watch the fire all serve as witnesses, too. The police officers arrest King and his gang as an ambulance arrives. Paramedics give Starr, DeVante, Seven, and Chris oxygen masks.

Maverick and Lisa tell Starr that they saw her throwing tear gas at the police on TV, calling her a "li'l radical." Maverick seems to approve of Chris more after knowing he stuck with Starr throughout the night, making plans to take Chris training with him at the boxing gym. Carlos tells the group that King will be convicted of arson, but will probably be out by the end of the week. DeVante offers to turn witness and let the police know where King's stash is, so he'll go to prison—protecting Kenya, Iesha, and the whole neighborhood.

Late next morning, Lisa wakes Starr up; Ms. Ofrah is on the phone. She apologizes for putting Starr in a dangerous situation and for the way the trial turned out, but also lets Starr know that she thinks she has a future in activism. Starr sees that Hailey texted her "I'm sorry," but when Starr asks Hailey what for, she realizes that Hailey isn't really apologizing but is only sorry about how Starr reacted. Starr decides to cut Hailey out of her life, since she has become a toxic friend.

Starr walks into the kitchen: Sekani is eating a sandwich, Maverick is cutting rose petals to plant a new bush, and Seven is unpacking kitchen plates. A picture of Starr throwing the tear gas can is on the front page of the newspaper; news channels all over the country are airing footage. Maverick and Lisa explain that even though money will be tight after the store's destruction, they can still make the new house work financially.

The family drives to the store to survey the damage. Their store and others on the street have been completely destroyed, but Mr. Lewis tells them that he is retiring and giving them his barber-shop property so that Maverick can expand the store when he renovates. Starr, her family, and some members of the community set to work on the store with gloves and garbage bags.

Starr looks up from working to see Kenya standing in front of her. Kenya explains that she and Lyric will move in with their grandmother, and that King beat Iesha; she had to go the hospital with a concussion, but she will recover soon. Kenya also apologizes for always referring to Seven as "her" brother rather than "our" brother, and Starr apologizes for never inviting Kenya to hang out with her Williamson friends because she was ashamed of where she lived. Kenya asks what will happen to the store, and Starr replies that they will rebuild it. She accepts that Khalil's story had an unhappy ending, but feels hope that the black community will continue to fight for justice. She promises makes a promise to the memory of Khalil that she will never forget him, will never give up, and will never be silent.

Analysis of Chapters 25 & 26

The destruction and rebirth of the store is a significant moment in the narrative of the Carter family. Maverick's store is inherently tied up with the family's identity; it represents their attempt to improve Garden Heights by providing goods for their community as well as offering jobs to those who need them to avoid the street life. Thus, the burning of the store even with its "black-owned" tag represents a culmination of the destructive nature of gang violence and the ways that disunity within the Garden Heights community ends up bringing the entire neighborhood down.

In contrast, however, the communal rebuilding of the store—punctuated by cries of encouragement from Garden Heights residents—represents the potential for unity moving forward. Mr. Lewis offers his own property to Maverick because he believes that there should be more men like him in the neighborhood: men focused on the broader movement for fighting oppression rather than inter-community violence from the highly polarized gangs. Like the burning of the store, the tragedy of Khalil's death has thus had unintentional positive consequences by bringing Garden Heights residents closer together.

Maverick's acceptance of Chris is a significant moment in terms of unity as well. Setting aside his innate parental protectiveness, Maverick seems to have come to terms with the fact that Starr's boyfriend being white does not mean that Maverick set a poor example for black men. In addition, the fact that Chris stuck by Starr's side throughout the night even though he had never been to Garden Heights before demonstrated the ability of support and love to overcome differences in background and racial differences.

The ending of the book explores how Starr has changed from the beginning. Her tragic experience has forever shaped her life; the images of her friends being killed can never be forgotten. Yet, Starr manages to remain positive. She even manages to keep up the spirit of the fight for justice, to use her horrific experiences as encouragement to continue to speak up against unfairness.

Readers can see how Starr has overcome internal struggles over the course of the novel. In the beginning, she was scared of speaking up and worried that her perspective wouldn't make a difference in the long run. Her vow at the end of the book never to be silent is indicative of her transformed viewpoint. There will always be injustice, but at the same time there will always be people willing to dedicate themselves to the struggle to make things right. Starr realizes that she can't fix the world singlehandedly, but she can use activism as a tool to fight injustice. Ultimately, she embraces the power of her voice and becomes intensely aware of its ability to make tangible, meaningful change.

The Hate U Give Symbols, Allegory and Motifs

Khalil's hairbrush (symbol)

Khalil's hairbrush is symbolic of the distrust that police officers have for minorities. One of the protest chants, "A hairbrush is not a gun!", represents the anger that the African-American community feels when it comes to the shooting of unarmed black people based on stereotypes, fear, and incomplete information. The hairbrush also invokes the 1999 death of Amadou Diallo. Police officers mistakenly believed that Diallo's wallet was a gun and fired 41 shots at him. Diallo's death led to an explosive controversy and national debate over racial profiling and police brutality.

Black Jesus (symbol)

Black Jesus is a symbol of the strength of African-Americans in the face of oppression. Maverick appropriates white-dominated Christianity by making Jesus black and leads his family in a group prayer each morning. The family derives strength from their prayer every day without relying on a white power or ideal. Black Jesus is also symbolic of the blended religion of Starr's family; Maverick, for example, does not approve of eating pork, which is a Muslim practice. The Carters frequently turn to Black Jesus for guidance while feeling pride for the strength of black people everywhere.

Thug Life (motif)

Tupac Shakur's concept of THUG LIFE—The Hate U Give Little Infants Fucks Everybody—is an important motif in the novel and the source of the book's title. Tupac's acronym explains the cyclical nature of poverty and crime that occurs as a result of an oppressive, racist social system. Starr and Khalil discuss the acronym shortly before Khalil's death, and Starr discusses Tupac's message with her father later on, coming to the conclusion that she can't be silent about the shooting. The acronym is symbolic of the struggles that black people in America face, emphasizing the generalizability of Starr's story. This motif runs throughout the entire novel, as characters such as DeVante and Khalil get caught up in a system that traps them.

Chris's Rolls Royce (symbol)

Chris's Rolls Royce is symbolic of his privilege, both financial and racial. Starr worries that the differences in her and Chris's backgrounds will prevent them from opening up completely to each other. She hides the parts of her life that she believes will make her appear "ghetto," including Natasha and Khalil's deaths. However, the symbol of white privilege as a barrier to their interracial relationship is inverted when Starr and Chris have an honest conversation about the need to accept each other inside of the very car that represents the differences between them.

The Fresh Prince of Bel-Air (allegory)

Starr's favorite TV show is *The Fresh Prince of Bel-Air*, which stars Will Smith and tells the story of a black teenager who is sent from his West Philadelphia neighborhood to live with his wealthy aunt and uncle in their mansion in Bel Air after he gets in a fight. Starr herself points out the allegorical nature of the show in regards to her own life. Just as Will was sent to Bel Air because of trouble in his neighborhood, Starr was sent to Williamson Prep after Natasha's death. However, the analogy doesn't extend to how comfortable Will and Starr feel in their respective new environments. Will still retains his own personality, while Starr feels the need to hide hers.

The Hate U Give Metaphors and Similes

"Natasha's mannequin wore a white dress with pink and yellow flowers all over it." (metaphor)

Starr uses the metaphor of a "mannequin" to describe Natasha's corpse. The metaphor helps her deal with the pain and unreality of seeing her best friend's lifeless body in the casket at her funeral. Similarly, she uses the metaphor of a mannequin to tell herself that she is not actually seeing Khalil's body at his funeral.

blubbering like a little kid who skinned her knee (simile)

This simile occurs when Starr heads back from the interview with the DA. The conversation is emotionally taxing on top of all the other problems going on in Starr's life, and she ends up vomiting and crying. Since Maverick responds by hugging Starr, this simile also reflects the continued importance of Maverick in Starr's life. Even though Maverick couldn't be there for Starr when she actually was a little kid who skinned her knee, now that he is back in her life he's determined to stay there and be as good of a father as he possibly can.

It seriously looks like the circus is setting up in town. (simile)

Starr uses the simile of a circus to describe the amount of media trucks that surround the courthouse. This simile reflects the national attention that cases of police shooting such as Khalil's receive. It also reflects how much Starr has to overcome to testify to the grand jury; she feels the pressure of an entire nation on her shoulders.

It sounds like the Fourth of July behind us: pop after pop after pop. (simile)

Starr compares the riots and violence following Khalil's death to fireworks at the Fourth of July. This is a striking comparison because it highlights the contrast between the sadness of this night and the happiness of a holiday. It also emphasizes the violence of the occasion by drawing a parallel between the flares and fireworks, which are extremely loud and often frightening.

A heat wave hits like the sun dropped in. (simile)

This simile compares the heat wave from King's makeshift bomb that envelops the store to the sun itself. It's a powerful comparison, because it highlights the danger and violence of King's action. It also foreshadows the utter destruction that will result from the fire.

The Hate U Give Irony

"hood rich"

Maverick's father, Adonis Carter, was a one of most notorious drug dealers and gangbangers in the city. His involvement in the drug trade made him a huge amount of money; pictures of Maverick as a child show him playing with jewels and furs. However, Carter neglected Maverick, and ended up going to prison, because of the very same involvement in drug dealing that enabled him to be financially successful. Starr later identifies this irony as "hood rich": King's house is hood rich because it is broken down and crumbling from the outside, but stocked with televisions and fine furniture on the inside.

Thug Life (situational irony)

The concept of THUG LIFE is ironic because it demonstrates the cyclical nature of violence. Inner-city men are poor and have nowhere to turn, so they join gangs to gain a sense of community and money—but because of the violence that accompanies gang life, these men often go to prison or end up dead, and thus leave their children with no choice but to join gangs. It's ironic that decisions made to improve one's life end up contributing to the endless loop of negativity.

Carlos and Maverick (situational irony)

Carlos and Maverick are constantly feuding, because Maverick resents the fact that Carlos was essentially Starr's father during the time that Maverick was in prison. The two men seem unaware that their constant fighting hurts Starr, making her feel stressed and guilty. By fighting over how to best make Starr happy, Carlos and Maverick inadvertently make her unhappy.

looting (situational irony)

The oppressive systems that keep minorities from advancing contribute to issues such as police brutality. After police shootings, anger bubbles over and Garden Heights residents riot, burning and looting their own stores. This contributes to a negative media stereotype that further perpetuates and justifies oppressive systems. The residents' expressions of their anger leads to further causes for anger.

The Hate U Give Imagery

Khalil's shooting

Khalil's shooting is described in tense language that emphasizes the terror and horror of the situation. Blood is described as spraying from Khalil's body as he jerks around; his eyes go lifeless when he passes away. The minimalist description, coupled with horrific imagery, clearly conveys the tragedy of the situation.

Chris's house

Chris's house is described with lavish adjectives; great attention is given to the paintings, furniture, and details of the large house. This detailed description conveys to the reader the extent of Chris's wealth and makes the contrast between Starr's house, and thus her background and experiences, very prominent. For example, Starr points out that her Garden Heights house could actually fit inside of Chris's house.

the riots

The riots on Magnolia are described using rich, descriptive language; the fire envelops the store like a sun, and the popping of objects hurled by the police reminds Starr of the Fourth of July. This language, in which the actions of the riots are compared to loud and intense things like the sun and fireworks, emphasizes the intensity of the emotions that surround the protests.

Emmett Till

The description of Emmett Till's body as so mutilated that people were not able to recognize him at first highlights the depravity of his death. Till's death in 1955 was only one in a series of racist killings that were truly horrific; race-based killings continue into the present; Khalil's fictional death has parallels in recent events in the U.S. By describing the extent of the damage to Till's body, the novel conveys the brutality of such senseless killings.

The Hate U Give Police Brutality and Black Lives Matter

Police brutality is the term for abuse of authority committed by police when they employ excessive force; it is particularly used in the context of unwarranted violence towards minorities. It is is usually applied to physical harm, but it can also include psychological harm through insults and intimidation. The modern definition of police brutality has its roots in the Civil Rights movement era, when police brutally put down peaceful protests in places like Selma, Alabama. In recent years, individuals who commit acts of police brutality may do so with the tacit approval of their larger departments or may be "bad apples," or rogue officers. They may also try to cover up the illegality of their actions.

The international activist moment Black Lives Matter (BLM) was created in response to such police brutality. The movement began in 2013 after the hashtag #BlackLivesMatter spread on Twitter following the acquittal of George Zimmerman, a white man, after he shot Trayvon Martin, an unarmed black teen. BLM gained national recognition for street protests following the police-perpetrated deaths of Michael Brown in Ferguson, Missouri and Eric Garner in New York City. Since Ferguson, the movement has protested the deaths of black men and women in police shootings and in police custody.

BLM is part of a larger, polarized national debate on police brutality and racial profiling. The slogan "All Lives Matter" gained popularity as a counter to BLM; it has been criticized for misunderstanding what Black Lives Matter means at the expense of minorities. After two police officers were shot in Ferguson, the hashtag Blue Lives Matter was popularized by supporters of the police.

The Hate U Give Literary Elements

Genre

young adult fiction

Setting and Context

The novel is set in the fictitious urban neighborhood of Garden Heights as well as the wealthier suburbs surrounding the city, circa 2017.

Narrator and Point of View

The narrator is Starr Carter, a 16-year-old African-American girl living in Garden Heights and attending Williamson Prep school. It's in the first-person viewpoint.

Tone and Mood

Starr's witty, sarcastic, and upbeat social commentary gives the novel an optimistic tone in the face of tragedy. However, the book also has undertones of anger at the oppressive systems that its characters must fight against each and every day.

Protagonist and Antagonist

The protagonist is Starr; the antagonists are Officer Cruise, King, and more broadly racism and gang violence in general.

Major Conflict

The major conflict is between Starr and herself as she struggles to speak up and fight for Khalil. Another major conflict occurs between the book's African-American characters and the racism and brutality they face.

Climax

The climax of the novel occurs when King sets Maverick's store on fire; ultimately, Starr and the others manage to escape, and King is arrested.

Foreshadowing

Starr's concern over what to do if a police car stops her foreshadows Khalil's subsequent shooting. The innate bad feeling that Starr and Lisa get about the police department's investigation into Officer Cruise foreshadows the jury's decision not to indict.

Understatement

Allusions

The novel's title, The Hate U Give, is an allusion to a Tupac song.

Imagery

Paradox

Parallelism

Metonymy and Synecdoche

Personification

The Hate U Give Links

Angie Thomas's official website

http://angiethomas.com/

This website offers a biography of Angie Thomas, information on her books and upcoming events, and a personal blog.

Talking With Angie Thomas, Author of the Best-selling YA Novel Inspired by Black Lives Matter

https://www.thecut.com/2017/03/angie-thomas-the-hate-u-give-interview-ya-novel.html

This interview with author Angie Thomas was conducted for *The Cut* magazine and touches on Black Lives Matter as well as the intersection of race and gender.

New Crop of Young Adult Novels Explores Race and Police Brutality

https://www.nytimes.com/2017/03/19/books/review/black-lives-matter-teenage-books.html?_r=0

This *New York Times* article places *The Hate U Give* in the context of other recently-released young adult novels that deal with themes of race and police brutality.

Balzer + Bray Prevails in 13-House Auction for YA Debut

https://www.publishersweekly.com/pw/by-topic/childrens/childrens-book-news/article/69501-balzer-bray-prevails-in-13-house-auction-for-ya-debut.html

This short article in *Publisher's Weekly* highlights the success of *The Hate U Give* by describing the bidding war that Thomas's book generated.

"The Hate U Give": Angie Thomas' sensational debut novel should be required reading for clueless white people

https://www.salon.com/2017/03/04/the-hate-u-give-angie-thomas-sensational-debut-novel-should-be-required-reading-for-clueless-white-people/

This article in *Salon* argues that *The Hate U Give* should be "required reading" for people who don't understand the complexity of race issues in America.

The Hate U Give Essay Questions

1. **In what ways does Starr cope with the tragedy of Khalil's death? How do these coping techniques reflect the influences on her life such as family, friends, and media?**

   At first, Starr turns to her family and her community to help cope with her feelings of anger and sadness. Starr's parents talk with her, take her out to eat, hug her, and try to help her through the difficult aftermath of the shooting. Visiting Khalil's grandmother also gives Starr a sense of closure more than attending Khalil's funeral which is marred by local rivalries. Eventually, however, Starr's coping mechanisms transition from reaction to outright action: she protests after the jury decision and uses her elevated platform as the witness of the shooting to conduct a powerful televised interview.

2. **What insights does this novel generate concerning the national debate over police brutality and racial profiling? Does it open new perspectives or explain any inconsistencies?**

   The novel provides a nuanced perspective on a hypothetical police shooting which offers insight into the character of the broader debate in the U.S. For example, the interview given by the officer's father and the responses that Starr gets to her own interview represent the "Blue Lives Matter" response to Black Lives Matter protests in the U.S. The anger and frustration experienced by Starr and her friends, who cannot seem to beat the racist and oppressive systems of the police, helps explain why violent riots occur after grand jury decisions in similar cases. The fact that Carlos is a police officer prevents an easy characterization of all policemen as corrupt. Because each character is represented as a full person acting within a broader social system, the novel denies any simple explanations of police brutality issues but offers insight into the motivations of various groups involved.

3. **What role does family play in the novel? In what ways are unconventional families portrayed? Discuss two other family besides Starr's.**

   Family is essential to Starr's experience of the world; everything from her job to her school has been influenced by the hopes her parents have for her own life. Starr's family demonstrates how caring can extend across multiple homes—Seven lives with Iesha and King, but clearly respects and loves his parents and siblings at Starr's house. Khalil's family demonstrates the importance of extended family such as grandmothers to raise children when the negative influences of drugs tear families apart. Nevertheless, Khalil remains dedicated to his mother—he sells drugs just to help her pay back a debt—which points to the enduring familial connection that persists despite hardships.

4. **How does Hailey respond to Starr's struggle over Khalil's death? Is this a reflection of society or white privilege as a whole, or can the influence of Hailey's personality be teased out of the way she reacts?**

Starr is bothered by Hailey's treatment of Khalil's death because Hailey refuses to demonstrate any empathy or to attempt to see the situation from Starr's point of view. Hailey certainly has a confrontational, overbearing personality; she always wants to be the leader in Starr's friend group and quickly grows defensive when Starr points out that she made a racist comment. Negative social factors, such as racial privilege, undoubtedly factor into Hailey's behavior as well. Hailey refuses to accept the fact that well-meaning people can make harmful racist remarks. She accepts a glossed-over stereotype of Khalil as a drug dealer and won't accept Starr's attempts to explain further.

5. **Discuss the importance of speaking up in the novel. In what ways does Starr grow when it comes to learning to use her voice to fight for the issues she is passionate about?**

The powerful closing lines of the novel demonstrate the centrality of speaking up to the story. A major plot point is Starr's how star deals with her grief, going from disbelief to anger to action. Starr channels her disappointment with brutal, racist police into activism. She is inspired to do so in part by Kenya, who points out that Khalil would have done the same for her. Starr comes to agree with Kenya and her father in their belief that speaking up, protest, and action are effective ways to ensure change.

The Hate U Give Quizzes

1. **What is the party were Starr and Khalil attending at the beginning of the novel?**
   A. Big D's Fourth of July party
   B. Big D's spring break party
   C. Big Mav's spring break party
   D. Kenya's birthday party

2. **What kind of talk did Starr's parents have with her when she was twelve?**
   A. "the birds and the bees," and what to do if she was stopped by the police
   B. how to work in Big Mav's store
   C. what to do if she was stopped by the police
   D. "the birds and the bees"

3. **Why is Starr afraid to tell her dad that she's dating Chris?**
   A. Chris's father doesn't get along with Maverick's father
   B. Chris is involved in a gang
   C. Maverick seems to look down on black people who date white people
   D. Chris abuses Starr

4. **Why does Lisa feel like she owes Ms. Rosalie something?**
   A. Ms. Rosalie is Lisa's mother
   B. Ms. Rosalie babysat Starr and Sekani when Maverick was in prison
   C. Ms. Rosalie paid for Lisa's college education
   D. Ms. Rosalie loaned Lisa money

5. **At the beginning of the book, why is Starr not speaking to Chris?**
   A. Chris made a racist remark about Khalil
   B. Chris refused to buy a condom
   C. Chris refused to have sex with Starr
   D. Chris pulled out a condom, even though Starr said she wasn't ready for sex

6. **Why does Starr think that the investigation into Khalil's shooting will not be fair?**
   A. the detectives ask her if Khalil sold narcotics
   B. the detectives refuse to ask her questions
   C. the detectives ask her what kind of party she and Khalil were leaving
   D. the detectives ask her if Khalil showed the officer his license and registration

7. **Why does Carlos punch Officer Cruise?**
   - A. Cruise punches him first
   - B. Cruise makes a racist remark about Khalil
   - C. Cruise makes a racist remark about Starr
   - D. Cruise pointed his gun at Starr

8. **What object did Officer Cruise believe to be a gun?**
   - A. an actual gun
   - B. a hairbrush
   - C. a cell phone
   - D. a wallet

9. **What is Starr's nickname?**
   - A. Crunch
   - B. Starry
   - C. Bunch
   - D. Munch

10. **Why does Starr get mad when Hailey and Maya protest Khalil's death?**
    - A. Hailey and Maya don't protest
    - B. they only protest because Starr tells them to
    - C. they mess up the words to the protest chant
    - D. they only protest so they can get out of class

11. **What does Starr see in the street while Maverick is weeding?**
    - A. a helicopter
    - B. a limousine
    - C. Officer Cruise's father
    - D. a tank

12. **Why does King want to kill DeVante?**
    - A. DeVante tried to shoot King
    - B. DeVante snitched on King to the police
    - C. King doesn't want to kill DeVante
    - D. DeVante stole money from King

13. **How do Kenya and Starr know each other?**
    - A. they share a brother, Sekani
    - B. they share a mother, Iesha
    - C. they share a sister, Lyric
    - D. they share a brother, Seven

14. **Why did Khalil sell drugs?**
    - A. he was trying to help Brenda pay a debt to King
    - B. he was trying to help DeVante pay King back
    - C. he was trying to help Lisa pay a debt to King
    - D. he was trying to make more money than King

15. **At the beginning of the book, how do people in Garden Heights refer to Starr?**
    A. "Sekani's sister who works in the clinic"
    B. "Kenya's sister who works in the store"
    C. "big Mav's daughter who works in the store"
    D. "Lisa's daughter who works in the clinic"

16. **When does Chris tell Starr that he knows she's the witness in Khalil's case?**
    A. the night of Big D's spring break party
    B. the night of junior prom
    C. the night of the riots
    D. the night of Starr's birthday party

17. **Who is Goon?**
    A. a Cedar Grove King Lord and King's friend
    B. a West Side King Lord and Maverick's friend
    C. a Garden Disciple and Maverick's friend
    D. a Cedar Grove King Lord and Maverick's friend

18. **Why did Hailey unfollow Starr's Tumblr?**
    A. Starr posted a picture of Martin Luther King, Jr.
    B. Starr posted a picture of Kenya
    C. Starr posted a picture of Khalil
    D. Starr posted a picture of Emmett Till

19. **Who is Iesha?**
    A. Sekani and Starr's mother
    B. Starr and Lyric's mother
    C. Sekani and Kenya's mother
    D. Seven and Kenya's mother

20. **When do the King Lords jump DeVante?**
    A. when he visits Dalvin's grave
    B. when he goes to Magnolia to protest
    C. when he visits his mother's grave
    D. when he goes to the park to sell drugs

21. **What does Starr throw at the police?**
    A. a Molotov cocktail
    B. her Jordans
    C. a bullhorn
    D. a can of tear gas

22. **Who sets Big Mav's store on fire?**
    A. DeVante
    B. Iesha
    C. King
    D. Starr

23. **Who created the acronym Thug Life?**
    A. Tupac Shakur
    B. Huey Newton
    C. Malcom X
    D. Kendrick Lamar

24. **What kind of career does Ms. Ofrah think Starr would be good at?**
    A. nurse
    B. lawyer
    C. activist
    D. professor

25. **Who gets in a fight at school?**
    A. Starr, Hailey, Remi, and Seven
    B. Starr, DeVante, Chris, and Maya
    C. Starr, Hailey, Chris, and Seven
    D. Starr, Hailey, Maya, and Sekani

Quiz 1 Answer Key

1. **(B)** Big D's spring break party
2. **(A)** "the birds and the bees," and what to do if she was stopped by the police
3. **(C)** Maverick seems to look down on black people who date white people
4. **(B)** Ms. Rosalie babysat Starr and Sekani when Maverick was in prison
5. **(D)** Chris pulled out a condom, even though Starr said she wasn't ready for sex
6. **(A)** the detectives ask her if Khalil sold narcotics
7. **(D)** Cruise pointed his gun at Starr
8. **(B)** a hairbrush
9. **(D)** Munch
10. **(D)** they only protest so they can get out of class
11. **(D)** a tank
12. **(D)** DeVante stole money from King
13. **(D)** they share a brother, Seven
14. **(A)** he was trying to help Brenda pay a debt to King
15. **(C)** "big Mav's daughter who works in the store"
16. **(B)** the night of junior prom
17. **(D)** a Cedar Grove King Lord and Maverick's friend
18. **(D)** Starr posted a picture of Emmett Till
19. **(D)** Seven and Kenya's mother
20. **(A)** when he visits Dalvin's grave
21. **(D)** a can of tear gas
22. **(C)** King
23. **(A)** Tupac Shakur
24. **(C)** activist
25. **(A)** Starr, Hailey, Remi, and Seven

The Hate U Give Quizzes

1. **What is the name of Starr's neighborhood?**
   A. Garden Heights
   B. Williamson
   C. Carnation
   D. Magnolia

2. **Who was in the "Hood Trio?"**
   A. Starr, Chris, and Maya
   B. Starr, Khalil, and Natasha
   C. Starr, Khalil, and Kenya
   D. Starr, Sekani, and Seven

3. **Who was Starr's father figure while Maverick was in jail?**
   A. Carlos
   B. King
   C. Goon
   D. Seven

4. **Why did Maverick leave his gang?**
   A. he became a father
   B. he got in trouble with King
   C. he was almost killed
   D. he was never in a gang

5. **Where does Lisa work?**
   A. a school
   B. a law office
   C. a clinic
   D. the store

6. **What does King do at Khalil's funeral?**
   A. put a green bandana on Khalil's body
   B. put a gray bandana on Khalil's body
   C. sets fire to the store
   D. throw a brick through the window

7. **Why is Starr afraid to go to Khalil's funeral?**
   A. she is afraid King will show up
   B. she doesn't want to see his body
   C. she doesn't want to cry in front of everyone
   D. she doesn't want to see his family

8. **Where do Starr and Seven go the morning after the first riots?**
   A. Magnolia, to protest Khalil's death
   B. the store, to help Maverick
   C. Rose Park, to play basketball
   D. Rose Park, to see DeVante

9. **What does DeVante ask Maverick for help with?**
   A. how to get King arrested
   B. how to leave his gang
   C. how to open a store
   D. how to drive a car

10. **Why do the King Lords target Mr. Lewis?**
    A. he said they burned a police car
    B. he was a Garden Disciple
    C. he implicated them on TV, and he was hiding DeVante
    D. he tried to get King arrested

11. **What is the name of the Tumblr that Starr makes to honor Khalil?**
    A. "The Real Khalil"
    B. "The Khalil I Know"
    C. "Thug Life"
    D. "The Hate U Give"

12. **Where does DeVante work?**
    A. Maverick's store
    B. Lisa's clinic
    C. Williamson Prep
    D. Just Us for Justice

13. **Who gives an interview defending Officer Cruise?**
    A. Detective Gomez
    B. the chief of police
    C. Carlos
    D. his father

14. **Why did King let Maverick leave the King Lords?**
    A. Maverick took a prison charge for King
    B. Maverick protected Iesha from the police
    C. Maverick gave King Lord a lot of money
    D. Maverick's father asked King to let him leave

15. **What does Starr say she wants to ask Officer Cruise during her television interview?**
    A. if he wishes that he shot her
    B. if he regrets shooting Khalil
    C. whether he would have shot Starr if she got out of the car
    D. whether he would have shot Khalil if Khalil were white

16. **What is Starr's favorite TV show?**
        A. "Empire"
        B. "The Fresh Prince of Bel-Air"
        C. "Breaking Bad"
        D. "Orange is the New Black"

17. **What are the names of Starr's brothers?**
        A. Sekani and Carlos
        B. DeVante and Sekani
        C. DeVante and Seven
        D. Seven and Sekani

18. **Why does Seven want to go to community college?**
        A. so he can protect Starr from King
        B. so he can stay with the King Lords
        C. it's the only college he was accepted to
        D. so he can protect his sisters and mother from King

19. **Who are Seven's parents?**
        A. Maverick and Lisa
        B. King and Iesha
        C. Maverick and Iesha
        D. King and Lisa

20. **How does Iesha help Seven?**
        A. she helps him take DeVante to the hospital
        B. she tells him to leave the house with Kenya, Lyric, and DeVante
        C. she tells him where King is on the night of the grand jury decision
        D. she goes to his high school graduation

21. **Why does Seven have to leave his Mustang?**
        A. it was set on fire
        B. its tires were slashed by King Lords
        C. he couldn't remember where he parked it
        D. it ran out of gas

22. **What is King arrested for?**
        A. arson
        B. murder
        C. assault
        D. selling drugs

23. **Who does Mr. Lewis give his store to?**
    A. King
    B. Starr
    C. DeVante
    D. Maverick

24. **Why is Carlos put on leave from the police force?**
    A. he punches Officer Cruise
    B. he quits
    C. he criticizes the police department
    D. he stops showing up to work

25. **Why does Kenya want Starr to speak up for Khalil?**
    A. Khalil would have done the same for Starr
    B. she thinks Starr is brave
    C. King forces her to
    D. she wants Starr to get famous

Quiz 2 Answer Key

1. **(A)** Garden Heights
2. **(B)** Starr, Khalil, and Natasha
3. **(A)** Carlos
4. **(A)** he became a father
5. **(C)** a clinic
6. **(B)** put a gray bandana on Khalil's body
7. **(B)** she doesn't want to see his body
8. **(C)** Rose Park, to play basketball
9. **(B)** how to leave his gang
10. **(C)** he implicated them on TV, and he was hiding DeVante
11. **(B)** "The Khalil I Know"
12. **(A)** Maverick's store
13. **(D)** his father
14. **(A)** Maverick took a prison charge for King
15. **(A)** if he wishes that he shot her
16. **(B)** "The Fresh Prince of Bel-Air"
17. **(D)** Seven and Sekani
18. **(D)** so he can protect his sisters and mother from King
19. **(C)** Maverick and Iesha
20. **(B)** she tells him to leave the house with Kenya, Lyric, and DeVante
21. **(D)** it ran out of gas
22. **(A)** arson
23. **(D)** Maverick
24. **(A)** he punches Officer Cruise
25. **(A)** Khalil would have done the same for Starr

The Hate U Give Quizzes

1. **What is the Nae-Nae?**
   - A. a type of dance
   - B. a type of drug
   - C. a type of car
   - D. a type of gang

2. **How old was Starr when Natasha died?**
   - A. 7
   - B. 16
   - C. 10
   - D. 18

3. **Where did Khalil work?**
   - A. Lisa's clinic
   - B. Reuben's
   - C. Garden Heights high school
   - D. Maverick's store

4. **Who is Khalil's brother?**
   - A. Cameron
   - B. Sekani
   - C. DeVante
   - D. Seven

5. **What is Chris's nickname for Starr?**
   - A. Fresh Princess
   - B. Moon
   - C. Starr-Starr
   - D. Honey Bunches of Oats

6. **Why are Starr and Lisa angry after leaving the police station?**
   - A. the detectives yelled at Starr
   - B. Starr never got a chance to talk
   - C. they think the investigation is already stacked against them
   - D. they think the investigation went very well

7. **When does King place a gray bandana on Khalil's body?**
   - A. at the crime scene
   - B. he doesn't
   - C. at the morgue
   - D. at his funeral

8. **What color is associated with the King Lords?**
    A. gray
    B. blue
    C. green
    D. black

9. **Who does Chris live near?**
    A. Starr
    B. Carlos
    C. Lisa
    D. Kenya

10. **Who started the Williamson Prep protest?**
    A. Hailey
    B. Chris
    C. Maya
    D. Remy

11. **What does Starr give to DeVante?**
    A. her books
    B. her old computer
    C. her old TV
    D. her dog

12. **Who gives Lisa and Maverick money for their down payment?**
    A. Seven
    B. Lisa's mother
    C. Carlos
    D. Mr. Lewis

13. **Who is in the "minority alliance"?**
    A. Kenya and Hailey
    B. Hailey and Starr
    C. Kenya and Maya
    D. Maya and Starr

14. **Who is Karen Monroe?**
    A. a detective
    B. defense attorney
    C. Starr's mother
    D. Just Us for Justice attorney

15. **What kind of car does Chris have for prom?**
    A. Mercedes Benz
    B. Ferrari
    C. Rolls Royce
    D. Lexus

16. **Who is Layla?**
    A. Kenya's younger sister
    B. Sekani's mother
    C. Seven's girlfriend
    D. DeVante's friend

17. **How long was Maverick in prison?**
    A. 5 years
    B. 3 years
    C. 6 months
    D. 10 years

18. **Who does Starr fight at school?**
    A. Hailey
    B. Jess
    C. Sekani
    D. Maya

19. **Where does Seven confront Iesha?**
    A. Garden Heights
    B. Maverick's store
    C. his high school graduation
    D. his birthday party

20. **Who is Dalvin?**
    A. Starr's friend
    B. DeVante's brother
    C. Maya's boyfriend
    D. Sekani's friend

21. **What side of Garden Heights does Starr live in?**
    A. east side
    B. south side
    C. north side
    D. west side

22. **Why does King burn Maverick's store?**
    A. Starr dry snitched on him
    B. King didn't burn the store
    C. Maverick threatened to kill Iesha
    D. Maverick is a Garden Disciple

23. **What sport does Starr play?**
    A. tennis
    B. soccer
    C. basketball
    D. softball

24. **How many brothers does Starr have?**
        A. 3
        B. 2
        C. she doesn't have any brothers
        D. 1

25. **Where does Carlos live?**
        A. the suburbs
        B. Williamson
        C. Garden Heights
        D. Magnolia

Quiz 3 Answer Key

1. **(A)** a type of dance
2. **(C)** 10
3. **(D)** Maverick's store
4. **(A)** Cameron
5. **(A)** Fresh Princess
6. **(C)** they think the investigation is already stacked against them
7. **(D)** at his funeral
8. **(A)** gray
9. **(B)** Carlos
10. **(D)** Remy
11. **(B)** her old computer
12. **(B)** Lisa's mother
13. **(D)** Maya and Starr
14. **(B)** defense attorney
15. **(C)** Rolls Royce
16. **(C)** Seven's girlfriend
17. **(B)** 3 years
18. **(A)** Hailey
19. **(D)** his birthday party
20. **(B)** DeVante's brother
21. **(D)** west side
22. **(A)** Starr dry snitched on him
23. **(C)** basketball
24. **(B)** 2
25. **(A)** the suburbs

The Hate U Give Quizzes

1. **What does bougie mean?**
   A. smelling weird
   B. aspiring to a higher social class
   C. very old
   D. a kind of weapon

2. **What kind of medical condition did Starr have?**
   A. asthma
   B. anemia
   C. peanut allergy
   D. diabetes

3. **What is King's nickname for Starr?**
   A. Munch
   B. Moon
   C. Fresh Princess
   D. Starr-Starr

4. **Who does the Carter family pray to?**
   A. Allah
   B. Jesus
   C. Black Jesus
   D. God

5. **Why does Starr panic on the way to the clinic?**
   A. a police car is behind Lisa's car
   B. a police car is behind Sekani's car
   C. a police car pulls Lisa over
   D. King is following Sekani

6. **What kind of food does Hailey make a racist comment about?**
   A. fried chicken
   B. collard greens
   C. pizza
   D. mac and cheese

7. **Who is Brenda?**
   A. Khalil's aunt
   B. Starr's aunt
   C. Lisa's sister
   D. Khalil's mom

8. **How did Starr get her name?**
    A. it's a nickname
    B. she was Maverick's light in the darkness
    C. Lisa chose it
    D. Carlos chose it

9. **What is Maverick's Harry Potter theory?**
    A. Harry Potter is about gangs
    B. Harry Potter is a King Lord
    C. Harry Potter is based on a Tupac song
    D. Harry Potter is nonfiction

10. **What kind of store does Mr. Lewis own?**
    A. barbershop
    B. grocery store
    C. general store
    D. deli

11. **What is Chris's favorite TV show?**
    A. "Seinfeld"
    B. "The Fresh Prince of Bel-Air"
    C. "Empire"
    D. "Friends"

12. **Who is Pam?**
    A. Starr's mother
    B. Lisa's sister
    C. Seven's mother
    D. Carlos's wife

13. **What is Carlos's job?**
    A. teacher
    B. working at Big Mav's store
    C. police officer
    D. nurse

14. **Who is Ms. April Ofrah?**
    A. Starr's attorney
    B. Cruise's attorney
    C. Khalil's aunt
    D. Lisa's colleague

15. **What is the timespan of the novel?**
    A. about 20 weeks
    B. about 9 weeks
    C. about 2 weeks
    D. about 13 weeks

16. **What college does Seven want to go to?**
        A. Harvard
        B. Howard
        C. Central Community
        D. he doesn't want to go to college

17. **What gets thrown through the Carters' window?**
        A. a bomb
        B. a brick
        C. a rock
        D. a knife

18. **How old is Starr?**
        A. 17
        B. 12
        C. 16
        D. 18

19. **The section titles are in the format of "X weeks after it." What is "it"?**
        A. Khalil's death
        B. Natasha's death
        C. Starr's interview
        D. Maya's death

20. **What item of clothing is Starr obsessed with?**
        A. jewelry
        B. skirts
        C. jeans
        D. sneakers

21. **What is the name of Starr's school?**
        A. Williamson Prep
        B. Riverside Prep
        C. Garden Heights High School
        D. Williamson Day

22. **What is a GD?**
        A. gangbanger
        B. Gang Disciple
        C. Garden Disciple
        D. Garden Den

23. **Where was Khalil shot?**
        A. Magnolia
        B. Carnation
        C. Big D's spring break party
        D. the suburbs

24. **Who is Rosalie?**
  - A. Khalil's grandmother
  - B. Starr's grandmother
  - C. Natasha's grandmother
  - D. Starr's friend

25. **What does Starr promise Khalil to never be?**
  - A. sad
  - B. angry
  - C. guilty
  - D. quiet

Quiz 4 Answer Key

1. **(B)** aspiring to a higher social class
2. **(A)** asthma
3. **(D)** Starr-Starr
4. **(C)** Black Jesus
5. **(B)** a police car is behind Sekani's car
6. **(A)** fried chicken
7. **(D)** Khalil's mom
8. **(B)** she was Maverick's light in the darkness
9. **(A)** Harry Potter is about gangs
10. **(A)** barbershop
11. **(B)** "The Fresh Prince of Bel-Air"
12. **(D)** Carlos's wife
13. **(C)** police officer
14. **(A)** Starr's attorney
15. **(D)** about 13 weeks
16. **(C)** Central Community
17. **(B)** a brick
18. **(C)** 16
19. **(A)** Khalil's death
20. **(D)** sneakers
21. **(A)** Williamson Prep
22. **(C)** Garden Disciple
23. **(A)** Magnolia
24. **(A)** Khalil's grandmother
25. **(D)** quiet

The Hate U Give Bibliography

Angie Thomas. <u>The Hate U Give</u>. New York, NY: Balzer + Bray, 2017.

Thomas, Angie. *The Hate U Give*. Balzer & Bray/Harperteen, 2017.

Angie Thomas. "Angie Thomas, author." Oct 20, 2017.
<<u>http://angiethomas.com/</u>>.

Dayna Evans. "Talking With Angie Thomas, Author of the Best-selling YA Novel Inspired by Black Lives Matter." <u>The Cut</u>. March 20, 2017. October 20, 2017. <<u>https://www.thecut.com/2017/03/angie-thomas-the-hate-u-give-interview-ya-novel.html</u>>.

Alexandra Alter. "New Crop of Young Adult Novels Explores Race and Police Brutality." <u>The New York Times</u>. March 19, 2017. October 20, 2017. <<u>https://www.nytimes.com/2017/03/19/books/review/black-lives-matter-teenage-books.html?_r=1</u>>.

Claire Kirch. "Balzer + Bray Prevails in 13-House Auction for YA Debut." <u>Publishers Weekly</u>. February 25, 2017. October 20, 2017. <<u>https://www.publishersweekly.com/pw/by-topic/childrens/childrens-book-news/article/69501-balzer-bray-prevails-in-13-house-auction-for-ya-debut.html</u>>.

Erin Keane. ""The Hate U Give": Angie Thomas' sensational debut novel should be required reading for clueless white people." <u>Salon</u>. March 4, 2017. October 20, 2017. <<u>https://www.salon.com/2017/03/04/the-hate-u-give-angie-thomas-sensational-debut-novel-should-be-required-reading-for-clueless-white-people/</u>>.

ClassicNotes

Gr▲deSaver™

Getting you the grade since 1999™

Other ClassicNotes from GradeSaver™

12 Angry Men	A Journal of the	Americanah
1984	Plague Year	American Beauty
8 1/2	Alas, Babylon	A Midsummer
Absalom, Absalom	A Lesson Before	Night's Dream
A Burnt-Out Case	Dying	A Modest Proposal
Accidental Death of	Alice in Wonderland	and Other Satires
an Anarchist	Alien	Amusing Ourselves
A Child Called "It"	All Creatures Great	to Death
A Christmas Carol	and Small	Anatomy of
A Clockwork	Allegiant	Criticism
Orange	Allen Ginsberg's	Andrew Marvell:
A Clockwork	Poetry	Poems
Orange (Film)	All My Sons	And Then There
A Confederacy of	All Quiet on the	Were None
Dunces	Western Front	An Enemy of the
Adam Bede	All the King's Men	People
A Doll's House	All the Light We	Angela's Ashes
A Farewell to Arms	Cannot See	An Ideal Husband
Agamemnon	All the Pretty Horses	Animal Farm
A Grain of Wheat	A Long Way Gone	An Inspector Calls
A Grave	A Lost Lady	Anna Karenina
A Hero of Our Time	Altered	Anne Bradstreet:
A Hunger Artist	Amadeus	Poems

For our full list of over 250 Study Guides, Quizzes,
Sample College Application Essays, Literature Essays and E-texts, visit:

www.gradesaver.com

ClassicNotes

GradeSaver™

Getting you the grade since 1999™

Other ClassicNotes from GradeSaver™

Anthem
Antigone
Antony and
    Cleopatra
A&P and Other
    Stories
A Passage to India
Apocalypse Now
A Psalm of Life
A Raisin in the Sun
Arcadia
Are You There God?
    It's Me, Margaret.
Aristotle:
    Nicomachean
    Ethics
Aristotle's Poetics
Aristotle's Politics
Arms and the Man
A Room of One's
    Own
A Room With a
    View

A Rose For Emily
    and Other Short
    Stories
Around the World in
    80 Days
A Sentimental
    Journey Through
    France and Italy
A Separate Peace
As I Lay Dying
A Streetcar Named
    Desire
Astrophil and Stella
A Study in Scarlet
As You Like It
A Tale of Two Cities
A Thousand
    Splendid Suns
Atlantia
Atlas Shrugged
Atonement

A Very Old Man
    With Enormous
    Wings
A View From the
    Bridge
A Vindication of the
    Rights of Woman
A White Heron and
    Other Stories
A Wrinkle in Time
Babbitt
Balzac and the Little
    Chinese
    Seamstress
Bartleby the
    Scrivener
Bastard Out of
    Carolina
Beloved
Benito Cereno
Beowulf
Between the World
    and Me

For our full list of over 250 Study Guides, Quizzes,
Sample College Application Essays, Literature Essays and E-texts, visit:

www.gradesaver.com

ClassicNotes

GradeSaver™

Getting you the grade since 1999™

Other ClassicNotes from GradeSaver™

Bhagavad-Gita
Billy Budd
Black Beauty
Black Boy
Black Skin, White Masks
Blade Runner
Bleak House
Bless Me, Ultima
Blindness
Blink
Blood Meridian: Or the Evening Redness in the West
Blood Wedding
Bluest Eye
Brave New World
Breakfast at Tiffany's
Breakfast of Champions
Burmese Days

By Night in Chile
Call of the Wild
Candide
Cane
Cannery Row
Casablanca
Catch-22
Catching Fire
Cathedral
Cat on a Hot Tin Roof
Cat's Cradle
Ceremony
Charlie and the Chocolate Factory
Charlotte's Web
Charlotte Temple
Childhood's End
Children of Men
Chinese Cinderella
Christina Rossetti: Poems
Christmas Bells

Christopher Marlowe's Poems
Chronicle of a Death Foretold
Citizen: An American Lyric
Citizen Kane
Civil Disobedience
Civilization and Its Discontents
Civil Peace
Cloud Atlas
Clueless
Coleridge's Poems
Comedy of Errors
Communist Manifesto
Confessions
Confessions of an English Opium Eater

For our full list of over 250 Study Guides, Quizzes,
Sample College Application Essays, Literature Essays and E-texts, visit:

www.gradesaver.com

ClassicNotes

GrAdeSaver™

Getting you the grade since 1999™

Other ClassicNotes from GradeSaver™

Connecticut Yankee in King Arthur's Court
Coriolanus
Crewel
Crime and Punishment
Crossed
Cry, the Beloved Country
Cymbeline
Cyrano de Bergerac
Daisy Miller
David Copperfield
Dead Poets Society
Death and the King's Horseman
Death and the Maiden
Death in Venice
Death of a Salesman
Democracy in America

Desiree's Baby
Desire Under the Elms
Devil in a Blue Dress
Dharma Bums
Disgrace
Divergent
Divine Comedy-I: Inferno
Do Androids Dream of Electric Sheep?
Doctor Faustus (Marlowe)
Dombey and Son
Don Quixote Book I
Don Quixote Book II
Dora: An Analysis of a Case of Hysteria
Dracula

Dr. Jekyll and Mr. Hyde
Dr. Strangelove
Dubliners
East of Eden
Edgar Huntly: Memoirs of a Sleep-Walker
Educating Rita
El Despertar
Electra by Sophocles
Emily Dickinson's Collected Poems
Emma
Ender's Game
Endgame
Enduring Love
Enrique's Journey
Equus
Esperanza Rising
Eternal Sunshine of the Spotlight Mind

For our full list of over 250 Study Guides, Quizzes,
Sample College Application Essays, Literature Essays and E-texts, visit:

www.gradesaver.com

ClassicNotes

GradeSaver™

Getting you the grade since 1999™

Other ClassicNotes from GradeSaver™

Ethan Frome
Eugene Onegin
Evangeline; A Tale of Acadie
Evelina
Everyday Use
Everyman: Morality Play
Everything is Illuminated
Exeter Book
Extremely Loud and Incredibly Close
Ezra Pound: Poems
Facundo: Or, Civilization and Barbarism
Fahrenheit 451
Fallen Angels
Fantastic Mr. Fox
Fantomina
Fear and Loathing in Las Vegas

Fences
Fifth Business
Fight Club
Fight Club (Film)
Flags of Our Fathers
Flannery O'Connor's Stories
Flight
Flowers for Algernon
Foe
For Colored Girls Who Have Considered Suicide When the Rainbow Is Enuf
For Whom the Bell Tolls
Founding Brothers
Frankenstein
Franny and Zooey
Freakonomics
Friday Night Lights

From the Mixed-Up Files of Mrs. Basil E. Frankweiler
Fun Home
Gargantua and Pantagruel
Gattaca
Gilead
Girl With a Pearl Earring
Goethe's Faust
Gone Girl
Gorilla, My Love
Go Set a Watchman
Go Tell it On the Mountain
Great Expectations
Green Grass, Running Water
Grendel
Gulliver's Travels
Hamlet

For our full list of over 250 Study Guides, Quizzes,
Sample College Application Essays, Literature Essays and E-texts, visit:

www.gradesaver.com

ClassicNotes

GrAdeSaver™

Getting you the grade since 1999™

Other ClassicNotes from GradeSaver™

Hard Times
Haroun and the Sea of Stories
Harriet the Spy
Harry Potter and the Cursed Child
Harry Potter and the Philosopher's Stone
Hatchet
Heart of Darkness
Hedda Gabler
Henry IV Part 1
Henry IV Part 2
Henry IV (Pirandello)
Henry V
Herzog
Hippolytus
Hiroshima
Holes
Homegoing
Homo Faber

House of Mirth
House on Mango Street
Howards End
How the Garcia Girls Lost Their Accents
How to Read Literature Like a Professor
I Am Malala
I, Claudius
I for Isobel
I Know Why the Caged Bird Sings
Iliad
Incidents in the Life of a Slave Girl
In Cold Blood
Inherit the Wind
In Our Time
Insurgent

Interpreter of Maladies
In the Heart of the Sea: The Tragedy of the Whaleship Essex
In the Penal Colony
In the Skin of a Lion
In the Time of the Butterflies
Into the Wild
Into Thin Air
Invisible Man
Ishmael
Island of the Blue Dolphins
It's Kind of a Funny Story
I Will Marry When I Want
James and the Giant Peach
Jane Eyre

For our full list of over 250 Study Guides, Quizzes,
Sample College Application Essays, Literature Essays and E-texts, visit:

www.gradesaver.com

ClassicNotes

GradeSaver™

Getting you the grade since 1999™

Other ClassicNotes from GradeSaver™

Jaws
Jazz
John Donne: Poems
Johnny Tremain
Jorge Borges: Short
   Stories
Joseph Andrews
Journey to the
   Center of the
   Earth
Jude the Obscure
Julius Caesar
July's People
Jungle of Cities
Juno and the
   Paycock
Kama Sutra
Kate Chopin's Short
   Stories
Keats' Poems and
   Letters
Kidnapped
Kindred

King Lear
King Solomon's
   Mines
Kokoro
Krik? Krak!
Kurt Vonnegut's
   Short Stories
La Campana de
   Cristal
Lady Audley's
   Secret
Lady Chatterley's
   Lover
Lady Windermere's
   Fan
La Edad de la
   Inocencia
La La Land
Lancelot: Or, the
   Knight of the Cart
Langston Hughes:
   Poems

Las Aventuras de
   Tom Sawyer
Last of the
   Mohicans
Leaves of Grass
Left to Tell
Legend
Le Morte d'Arthur
Les Miserables
Letter From
   Birmingham Jail
Let the Circle be
   Unbroken
Leviathan
Libation Bearers
Lies My Teacher
   Told Me
Life is Beautiful
Life of Pi
Light In August
Like Water for
   Chocolate
Little Women

For our full list of over 250 Study Guides, Quizzes,
Sample College Application Essays, Literature Essays and E-texts, visit:

www.gradesaver.com

ClassicNotes

GrAdeSaver™

Getting you the grade since 1999™

Other ClassicNotes from GradeSaver™

For our full list of over 250 Study Guides, Quizzes, Sample College Application Essays, Literature Essays and E-texts, visit:

www.gradesaver.com

ClassicNotes

GradeSaver™

Getting you the grade since 1999™

For our full list of over 250 Study Guides, Quizzes,
Sample College Application Essays, Literature Essays and E-texts, visit:

www.gradesaver.com

ClassicNotes

GradeSaver™

Getting you the grade since 1999™

Other ClassicNotes from GradeSaver™

Perfume: The Story
of a Murderer
Persepolis: The
Story of a
Childhood
Persuasion
Phaedra
Phaedrus
Pilgrim's Progress
Poems of W.B.
Yeats: The Rose
Poems of W.B.
Yeats: The Tower
Poe's Poetry
Poe's Short Stories
Poetry
Politics and the
English Language
Pope's Poems and
Prose
Portrait of the Artist
as a Young Man
Pretty Woman

Pride and Prejudice
Private Memoirs and
Confessions of a
Justified Sinner
Prometheus Bound
Psycho
Pudd'nhead Wilson
Purple Hibiscus
Pygmalion
Rabbit, Run
Rashomon
Ray Bradbury: Short
Stories
Reached
Reading Lolita in
Tehran
Rear Window
Rebecca
Reflections on
Gandhi
Regeneration
Return of the Native
Rhinoceros

Richard II
Richard III
Riders to the Sea
Rip Van Winkle and
Other Stories
Robert Browning:
Poems
Robert Frost: Poems
Robinson Crusoe
Roll of Thunder,
Hear My Cry
Roman Fever and
Other Stories
Romeo and Juliet
Romeo and Juliet
(Film 1968)
Roots
Rope
Rosencrantz and
Guildenstern Are
Dead
Rudyard Kipling:
Poems

For our full list of over 250 Study Guides, Quizzes,
Sample College Application Essays, Literature Essays and E-texts, visit:

www.gradesaver.com

ClassicNotes

GradeSaver™

Getting you the grade since 1999™

ClassicNotes

GradeSaver™

Getting you the grade since 1999™

Other ClassicNotes from GradeSaver™

The Caucasian Chalk Circle
The Cherry Orchard
The Children's Hour
The Chocolate War
The Chosen
The Chrysalids
The Chrysanthemums
The Circle
The Clash of Civilizations
The Collector
The Color of Water
The Color Purple
The Consolation of Philosophy
The Conversation
The Coquette
The Count of Monte Cristo

The Country of the Pointed Firs and Other Stories
The Country Wife
The Cricket in Times Square
The Crucible
The Crying of Lot 49
The Curious Incident of the Dog in the Night-time
The Day Is Done
The Death Cure
The Death of Ivan Ilych
The Devil and Tom Walker
The Devil's Arithmetic

The Diary of a Young Girl by Anne Frank
The Drover's Wife
The Duchess of Malfi
The Dumb Waiter
The Electric Kool-Aid Acid Test
The Emperor of Ice Cream
The English Patient
The Epic of Gilgamesh
The Eumenides
The Faerie Queene
The Fall of the House of Usher
The Fault in Our Stars
The Federalist Papers
The Fish

For our full list of over 250 Study Guides, Quizzes,
Sample College Application Essays, Literature Essays and E-texts, visit:

www.gradesaver.com

ClassicNotes

GradeSaver™

Getting you the grade since 1999™

Other ClassicNotes from GradeSaver™

The Five People You
Meet in Heaven
The Flowers of Evil
The Fountainhead
The French
Lieutenant's
Woman
The Frogs
The Garden Party
The Girl on the
Train
The Giver
The Glass Castle
The Glass
Menagerie
The Godfather
The God of Small
Things
The Golden Ass
The Good Earth
The Good Woman
of Setzuan
The Graduate

The Grapes of Wrath
The Great Gatsby
The Great Gatsby
(2013 Film)
The Guest
The Handmaid's
Tale
The Hate U Give
The Haunting of Hill
House
The Heart of the
Matter
The Help
The Hiding Place
The History Boys
The History of
Rasselas: Prince
of Abissinia
The History of
Sexuality, Vol. 1
The History of Tom
Jones, a
Foundling

The Hobbit
The Homecoming
The Hot Zone
The Hound of the
Baskervilles
The House of
Bernarda Alba
The House of the
Seven Gables
The House of the
Spirits
The Hunger Games
The Iceman Cometh
The Idea of Order at
Key West
The Importance of
Being Earnest
The Infinite Sea
The Interlopers
Their Eyes Were
Watching God
The Island of Dr.
Moreau

For our full list of over 250 Study Guides, Quizzes,
Sample College Application Essays, Literature Essays and E-texts, visit:

www.gradesaver.com

ClassicNotes

GradeSaver™

Getting you the grade since 1999™

Other ClassicNotes from GradeSaver™

The Jew of Malta
The Joy Luck Club
The Jungle
The Kill Order
The Kite Runner
The Lais of Marie
de France
The Legend of
Sleepy Hollow
The Library of
Babel
The Life of Olaudah
Equiano
The Lightning Thief
The Lion and the
Jewel
The Lion, the Witch
and the Wardrobe
The Lone Ranger
and Tonto
Fistfight in
Heaven

The Lord of the
Rings: The
Fellowship of the
Ring
The Lord of the
Rings: The Return
of the King
The Lord of the
Rings: The Two
Towers
The Lottery and
Other Stories
The Lovely Bones
The Love Song of J.
Alfred Prufrock
The Magician's
Nephew
The Maltese Falcon
(1941 Film)
The Man in the High
Castle
The Man of Mode

The Marrow of
Tradition
The Master and
Margarita
The Mayor of
Casterbridge
The Maze Runner
The Metamorphosis
The Mill on the
Floss
The Monk
The Monkey's Paw
The Moonlit Road
and Other Ghost
and Horror
Stories
The Moonstone
The Most
Dangerous Game
The Murder of
Roger Ackroyd
The Namesake

For our full list of over 250 Study Guides, Quizzes,
Sample College Application Essays, Literature Essays and E-texts, visit:

www.gradesaver.com

ClassicNotes

GradeSaver™

Getting you the grade since 1999™

Other ClassicNotes from GradeSaver™

The Rocking-Horse
   Winner
The Rover
The Sandman
The Satanic Verses
The Scarlet Ibis
The Scarlet Letter
The Scarlet
   Pimpernel
The School for
   Scandal
The Scorch Trials
The Seagull
The Second Sex
The Secret Life of
   Bees
The Secret River
The Shack
The Shining
The Sign of the Four
The Silver Sword
The Snow Man
The Social Contract

The Sociological
   Imagination
The Sorrows of
   Young Werther
The Souls of Black
   Folk
The Sound and the
   Fury
The Sound of Waves
The Sovereignty and
   Goodness of God
The Spanish
   Tragedy
The Spirit Catches
   You and You Fall
   Down
The Steeple-Jack
The Story of My
   Life
The Storyteller
The Stranger
The Sun Also Rises

The Talented Mr.
   Ripley (Film)
The Taming of the
   Shrew
The Tempest
The Testing
The Theory of
   Moral Sentiments
The Things They
   Carried
The Threepenny
   Opera
The Tiger's Wife
The Time Machine
The Tortilla Curtain
The Trials of
   Brother Jero
The Trouble With
   Normal
The Truman Show
The Turn of the
   Screw
The Valley of Fear

For our full list of over 250 Study Guides, Quizzes,
Sample College Application Essays, Literature Essays and E-texts, visit:

www.gradesaver.com

ClassicNotes

GradeSaver™

Getting you the grade since 1999™

Other ClassicNotes from GradeSaver™

Under the Feet of
 Jesus
Untouchable
Up From Slavery
Ursula Le Guin:
 Short Stories
Utilitarianism
Utopia
Vanity Fair
Vanka
Villette
Volpone
Waiting for Godot
Waiting for Lefty
Waiting for the
 Barbarians
Walden
Walled States,
 Waning
 Sovereignty

Walt Whitman:
 Poems
War and Peace
Washington Square
We
Weep Not, Child
We Need New
 Names
What is the What
W. H. Auden:
 Poems
Where Are You
 Going, Where
 Have You Been?
Where the Red Fern
 Grows
White Fang
White Noise
White Teeth
Who's Afraid of
 Virginia Woolf

Wide Sargasso Sea
Wieland
Wilfred Owen:
 Poems
Winesburg, Ohio
Wise Blood
Women in Love
Wonder
Wordsworth's
 Poetical Works
Woyzeck
Wuthering Heights
Year of Wonders
Yonnondio: From
 the Thirties
Young Goodman
 Brown and Other
 Hawthorne Short
 Stories
Zeitoun
Z For Zachariah

For our full list of over 250 Study Guides, Quizzes,
Sample College Application Essays, Literature Essays and E-texts, visit:

www.gradesaver.com

23078328R00061

Made in the USA
Columbia, SC
02 August 2018